The Knitted Rug

The Knitted Rug

21 Fantastic Designs

Donna Druchunas

LARK BOOKS

A Division of Sterling Publishing Co., Inc.
New York

Editors: Marcianne Miller, Deborah Morgenthal
Art Director: Tom Metcalf
Associate Art Director: Shannon Yokeley
Photographer: Keith Wright
Cover Designer: Barbara Zaretsky
Illustrator: Orrin Lundgren
Assistant Editors: Nathalie Mornu, Rebecca Guthrie
Editorial Assistance: Delores Gosnell,
Rosemary Kast, Jeff Hamilton

Dedication

For my grandmother, Ruth Tolen, who taught me how to knit and who truly believed everything her grandchildren made was "bee-you-tee-ful"

The Library of Congress has cataloged the hardcover edition as follows:

Druchunas, Donna.
    The knitted rug : 21 fantastic designs / Donna Druchunas.
        p. cm.
    Includes bibliographical references and index.
    ISBN 1-57990-424-6
    1. Rugs. 2. Knitting- -Patterns. I. Title.
TT850. D78 2004
746.74- -dc22

                    2004005784

10 9 8 7 6 5 4 3 2

Published by Lark Books, A Division of
Sterling Publishing Co., Inc.
387 Park Avenue South, New York, N.Y. 10016

First Paperback Edition 2005
Text © 2004, Donna Druchunas
Photography & illustrations © 2004, Lark Books

Distributed in Canada by Sterling Publishing,
c/o Canadian Manda Group, 165 Dufferin Street
Toronto, Ontario, Canada M6K 3H6

Distributed in the United Kingdom by GMC Distribution Services,
Castle Place, 166 High Street, Lewes, East Sussex, England BN7 1XU

Distributed in Australia by Capricorn Link (Australia) Pty Ltd., P.O. Box 704, Windsor, NSW 2756 Australia

If you have questions or comments about this book, please contact:
Lark Books, 67 Broadway, Asheville, NC 28801
(828) 253-0467

Manufactured in China

The design in the rug on page 106 has been adapted from *Knitting in the Old Way: Designs and Techniques from Ethnic Sweaters*, by Priscilla Gibson-Roberts and Deborah Robson, by permission of Nomad Press.

ISBN 13: 978-1-57990-424-1 (hardcover) 978-1-57990-747-1 (paperback)
ISBN 10: 1-57990-424-6 (hardcover) 1-57990-747-4 (paperback)

For information about custom editions, special sales, premium and corporate purchases, please contact
Sterling Special Sales Department at 800-805-5489 or specialsales@sterlingpub.com.

table of contents

introduction

Until last year, I had never heard of or seen a knitted rug. Today, they cover my floors, decorate my walls, and fill my days.

As I've worked on the rugs in this book, I've explored my creativity, draped beautiful yarns all around my house, learned new (and old!) techniques, and experimented with design ideas by swatching. Knitting rugs has helped me to remember the relaxation that comes with the rhythm of simple knitting and to rediscover the satisfaction of creating beautiful gifts for myself and others.

Knitting rugs is an easy and satisfying way to learn how to knit.
Photo by Beverly Flaven

While sweaters, caps, and afghans warm one person at a time, rugs warm whole families. Unlike knitted garments whose fate is determined by fashion-show trends, the classic designs of knitted rugs are timeless. A hand-knit rug made in the 18th century looks just as comfortable in a sleek modern penthouse, a mountain cabin, or a cozy family home as it did on the rough-hewn floor of a country farmhouse.

My friends thought I was crazy when I told them I was writing a book about knitted rugs. "How can you knit a rug?" they'd ask. But every single visitor to my house falls in love with my rugs. As soon as they see the carpets, mats, runners and throws that have overtaken my home, they ask me if they, too, can knit a rug. My answer is, "Of course!" They leave with a list of supplies and find themselves at our local yarn shop, happily perusing new yarns and color combinations.

Rugs present a stress-free way to learn to knit. Even if you know only how to cast on and do the knit stitch, you can create stylish and functional rugs for your home. If you're an experienced knitter looking for a challenge, knitting rugs will add new skills to your knitting toolkit as you create distinctive works of beauty. Since rugs are simple shapes, there are no armholes or necklines to shape, no buttonholes to remember, and no constant measuring to ensure proper fit. You can use your precious knitting time to slow down and let your hands memorize the motions. Like me, maybe you'll find knitting rugs becomes your favorite form of meditation.

The Knitted Rug includes information for knitters of all levels:

☛ If you're curious or looking for inspiration, the first section covers the history of hand-knit rugs from ancient times up to the present day, with photos of rugs from museum collections, vintage knitting books, and contemporary fiber artists.

☛ If you're a new knitter or you're ready to learn new skills, the second section includes basic knitting lessons plus instructions for special rugmaking techniques, how to make embellishments and accessories, and how to finish rugs so they look wonderful and last a lifetime.

☛ If you're ready to jump in and start knitting a rug, the final section includes patterns for a collection of rugs with step-by-step instructions. I've also included design tips in each project to help get your creative juices flowing.

The rugs I've designed range from rough-and-tumble durable doormats to cuddly throws. Some rugs are knit, then felted, making them all but indestructible. Others are soft, serving as nap rugs for children, yoga mats, lap blankets, and wall hangings. You'll find large and small rugs, and some that can go either way. There are lined rugs, coiled rugs, and rugs like patchwork quilts. Many rugs are rectangular, others are square, oval, and round—and there are lots of tassels and fringe and other lovely touches to make the edges of them sensational.

Although I'm not a scholar or historian, I spent a fascinating year tracing the varied paths of knitted rugs—searching libraries, museums, antique shops, and the Internet. Every moment of my journey was fun. The first time I saw the Shakers' exquisite circular knitted rugs in a magazine article, I was hooked. From that day, through all of my research, and as I wrote every page, I've found myself enchanted by rug knitters around the world and the creative rug designs of the past and present.

Knitting rugs is enchanting. The way a single strand of yarn, twisted, looped, and pulled through itself by my hands becomes a beautiful, sturdy rug always amazes me. As you turn these pages, I hope you, too will be enchanted by the world of knitted rugs. May you pick up your knitting needles and start your knitted rug today!

My grandmother, Ruth Tolen, taught me to knit.
Photo by Alan Tolen

Suzann Thompson's circular garter stitch rug was the first modern-day knitted rug that came across my path. Its bright colors in simple stitches inspired me to start experimenting with designing my own rugs and, eventually, led to this book.
Photo by Dominic Cotignola

the history of hand-knit rugs

Knitters around the world have been making rugs for centuries. Found in folk art, popular craft, and professional textile traditions, rugs have always had a place in the knitter's repertoire. Using a variety of materials and techniques, knitters have fashioned many styles of rug: from ornate medieval knitted tapestries and humble rag rugs knitted by early Americans, to modern art-knitting and home décor items on department store shelves.

ANCIENT ROOTS

The English words "rug" and "carpet" are derived from the ancient Scandinavian rögg, meaning fleece, and the Latin carpere, meaning to card or pluck wool. In the United States today, carpets are usually room-sized floor coverings, while rugs are smaller decorative items. In Australia and Britain, the word rug is also sometimes used to refer to afghans and blankets.

Rugs were mentioned as early as the Greek Odyssey, when Homer spoke of drawing up a rug-covered stool for Ulysses to sit on. The word he used for rug meant animal fleece. In time, people started imitating the shaggy surface of an animal hide by making shag and pile rugs out of

Combining colors and textures can turn even a rug knit with basic Garter Stitch into an extraordinary design. Textile artist Judy Dercum knit intarsia color blocks and combined yarns in variegated and solid colors with a unique "tail-spun" yarn that looks like raw fleece from the sheep's back. The wild and wooly result is reminiscent of the earliest fleece rugs. *Photo by Dominic Cotignola*

loose wool attached to a woven background.

The ryas of northern Scandinavia and the knotted pile rugs of Asia were the first true rugs, woven with short pieces of yarn, or pile, knotted onto the backing to created a plush surface. The earliest known example, found at Pazyryk in Siberia, dates from the second- or third-century BCE.

Knitting and rug making followed similar paths—though separated in time—from origins in Arab lands to Europe and, later, to America.

The earliest items knit with the two-needle technique we use today are blue-and-white cotton stockings and fabric fragments from Islamic Egypt (1200-1500 CE) and two cushions found in the Castilian royal tomb in northern Spain (late 13th century). The stockings and cushions were knit at a very fine gauge and are decorated with stranded color work patterns and Arabic lettering. Their complexity and craftsmanship prove that knitting was already a highly developed craft.

Once knitting and rugs came together, knitters learned how to imitate existing rugmaking techniques and developed new styles of rugs unique to knitting.

MEDIEVAL MASTERPIECES

The earliest known knitted rugs are also the most elaborate. Large, pictorial carpets, known as Masterpieces, were knit by men seeking entrance into the knitting guilds in the Alsace region between Germany and France during the 17th and 18th centuries. These carpets range from beautiful to bizarre, each one an elaborate example of color work the like of which we will probably never see again. From flowers and Bible scenes to scripture texts and portraits of nobles, the minute details of these carpets provide clear evidence of the advanced skills of the knitters. At six feet (2 m) long, these rugs were much too heavy to knit with two straight knitting needles.

This color-work design by Lucy Neatby, knit at a fine gauge in many colors, was inspired by traditional woven Ashanti fabrics.
Photo by Dominic Cotignola

The knitters probably used several long double-pointed needles or a knitting frame (a precursor to the knitting machine, similar to a jumbo-sized version of the spools used to make knitted cord).

In medieval times, professional knitting was man's work. Only widows taking over their deceased husbands' memberships were allowed to join guilds. However, women in rural areas and convents also knit. One spectacular masterpiece, depicting Adam and Even in the Garden of Eden surrounded by many animals, was made by a group of nuns as a birthday gift for their bishop.

Not intended for use on the floor, medieval carpets were used as table runners and wall hangings.
Photo courtesy of Victoria & Albert Museum

With 20 or more colors, the medieval master-pieces are as complex as machine-woven tapestries. Charts, or graphs, similar to those we still use for color-work projects, were most likely used to keep track of the patterns. Knitters stranded unused colors across the back of the work, or wove them in, the way you'd knit the two-color Fair Isle In-the-Round project on page 103. Today, we knit pictorial designs using the Intarsia technique, with each block of color using a separate ball of yarn. (See the Thunderbird Intarsia Tapestry on page 106.) Intarsia uses less yarn and creates a lighter, more flexible fabric that is better suited to clothing. However, for knitted rugs, the extra strands on the back of the work add strength and have no disadvantage.

Some masterpieces were also fulled, or felted to increase their durability. Special felting houses provided large workspaces where artisans beat wet rugs with sticks, or stomped them with their feet, to cause the fibers to mat. Sometimes the dry felted rug was brushed with teasels (the dried seed heads of a thistle-like plant) to raise the nap, and then sheared with large scissors to create a smooth surface. In several master-pieces, the stitches are nearly invisible except where the surface has started to wear out.

EARLY AMERICAN CLASSICS

As the last knitted carpets of the Alsace guilds were being made, an entirely different type of knitted rug appeared in the United States and Canada. Made from strips of worn-out clothing, early rag rugs might seem to modern eyes to be products of frugal living. In truth, covering a floor with a rug—even one made from recycled rags—was an extravagance that few early Americans could afford. Yarn was too valuable to use for rug knitting. Because mill-spun yarn was expensive and hand spinning was so labor-intensive, yarn was used only for necessities such as hand-knit mittens and socks or woven cloth for new clothes.

The first rugs made in the New World were narrow strips of Garter Stitch, knit at a firm gauge, then sewn together. Color schemes were limited by the materials at hand and by the use of natural dyes. Experienced knitters worked out the patterns as they went along, and passed down their knowledge as oral tradition, like favorite family recipes.

Early American knitters created several different styles of knitted rugs. These designs continue to provide inspiration for new rugs, including many of the projects I designed for this book.

The simplest rectangular rugs ranged from randomly colored "hit-or-miss" rugs to preplanned stripe and checkerboard designs.

Quick-Knit Garter Stitch Rug (page 59) was inspired by early American American rag rugs.

Coiled or spiral rugs were made from long, thin strips of Garter Stitch. Beginning with two or three stitches, the knitting increased slowly over several feet and was coiled to form a circular center. The body of the rug grew like a snail, shaped from one long knitted strip. The rug ended with a decrease section, reversing the shaping used in the center.

Pinwheel rugs were knit in one piece. Twelve pie-slice sections shaped with short rows were worked around a center pivotal stitch. These pinwheels were sometimes surrounded by concentric circles sewn around the outside edge to create larger rugs resembling bulls-eyes. The center of a bulls-eye rug might also be a small coil or a gathered strip of Garter Stitch.

Oval rugs used techniques similar to bulls-eye rugs. A single strip of Garter Stitch, with shaped ends or folded in half lengthwise and sewn end to end, forms an oblong center, with longer strips sewn around the outside edge.

Handspun Oval (page 68) is a contemporary version of one that might have been made from patterned fabric in young girls' dresses.

The Knit-and-Purl Hearth Rug (page 77) is an updated design combining Garter Stitch and Stockinette Stitch strips in solid colors and stripes.

Simple Shaker Pinwheel (page 61) is a simplified design inspired by early pinwheel rugs.

The simple designs of Shaker crafts were inspired by their religious laws, which stipulated that "carpets are admissible, but they ought to be used with discretion, and made plain...The carpets in one room should be as near alike as can consistently be provided." A spirit message, or vision, also instructed knitters that "two colors are sufficient for one carpet. Make one strip of red and green, another of drab and gray, another of butternut and gray."

Many of the surviving Shaker rugs were knit by Sister Elvira Hulett in the late 19th century, when strict guidelines of simplicity were loosening. Her skills, which combine weaving, knitting, and braiding, reflect the long history of Shaker fiber arts.

Berber Rya Rug (page 90) is descended from Norse ryas and Asian knotted pile carpets, imitated in knitting by early American women.

Pile, or shag rugs were made using both yarn and fabric. Sturdy string was knit in Garter Stitch with 2"/5cm strips of yarn or fabric folded over every-other stitch on wrong-side rows to create a fluffy, yet durable, surface.

SHAKER AND AMISH ARTISANS

The best-known American folk-art rugs were made by two religious groups dedicated to doctrines of simple living.

The Shakers, arriving in America from England in 1774, created plain, yet elegant, styles of architecture, furniture, and handicrafts including knitted rugs. While Shaker communities are all but non-existent today, the classic lines of their designs continue to influence modern artisans.

By Colonial times, knitting had become women's work. Although women filled leadership roles in Shaker communities, chores were still divided along traditional gender lines. Still, Shaker Sisters had the opportunity to rotate among different jobs and to practice several crafts. Most of the surviving Shaker rugs combine knitting with other techniques, such as braiding or rug hooking.

By using multiple strands of yarn to blend colors, and by adding color-work designs to the Garter Stitch strips, Shaker Sister Elvira knit many elaborate rugs.
Photo courtesy of Shaker Museum and Library, Old Chatham, New York

Antique handmade rugs, such as this pile-knit rug, are frequently attributed to Shakers, but without documentation it is impossible to prove if they were truly made by Shaker Sisters.
Photo courtesy of Allan Arthur Cyber Rug Center

Like the Shakers, the Amish also designed rugs using a combination of techniques, as this rug with a braided center and Garter Stitch border shows.
Photo courtesy of Priscilla Gibson-Roberts, Heritage Museum

The Amish, another simple-living American religious group, still have thriving contemporary communities in the United States and in Canada. Amish women adopted rag rug techniques from popular books and continued to knit rugs long after the craft had gone out of favor in mainstream America.

Amish knitted rugs, made from alternating strips of knitting and braids, are often mistaken for crochet by non-knitters. Amish knitters often combined sections knit with lightweight fabrics (such as broadcloth from women's blouses) with braids made from heavier cloth (such as denim from men's work pants). Because Garter Stitch makes a heavy, dense fabric, the thickness of the knitting was equal to the thickness of the braid, creating a sturdy rug.

Like the early Shakers, the Amish saw rugs as no-frills functional objects. Yet women found ways to express artistic creativity by combining colors and shapes into distinctive patterns. Somber and dark colors from women's dresses predominate in many older designs, with brighter colors from children's clothes used as accents.

Amish oval and round rugs with braided or Garter Stitch centers surrounded by strips of Garter Stitch still inspire contemporary designers.
Photo courtesy of Priscilla Gibson-Roberts, Heritage Museum

Because its plush surface was so luxurious, early 20th-century knitting writers considered pile knitting to be the "king" of rug knitting techniques.
Photo courtesy of Allan Arthur Cyber Rug Center

FROM FOLK ART TO CONTEMPORARY REVIVAL

From Victorian times through the 20th century, knitting—and knitted rugs—developed as a folk craft with traditional regional designs. It also grew eventually, with ebbs and tides of interest, into a popular craft with patterns circulating among far-flung knitters through printed books and magazines.

In early magazines, since most women knew how to knit, the instructions were vague. Standardized knitting terminology was still in the infant stages, lacking today's "user-friendly" charts and terms. Thanks to a few books published in the early 20th century, instructions for knitting several old-style rugs have been preserved, but many undocumented techniques have very likely been lost forever.

Step-by-step patterns for rugs began showing up regularly in knitting books and magazines during the 1940s. Until this time, knitted rugs had been made with Garter Stitch, but after WWII, knitters and designers began experimenting with different stitch patterns, colors, and shaping techniques.

By the 1960s and 70s, the world of handcrafts had changed—instructions for traditional knitted rag rugs were hard to find, and the handing down of traditional folk-art techniques was largely a thing of memory. Designs for rugs made with yarn, rather than rags, cropped up in rug-making books from popular publishers such as *McCall's* and *Better Homes and Gardens* but the combi-

nation of crafts prevalent in Shaker and Amish rugs was disappearing. Influenced by the popularity of macramé, modern architecture, and other contemporary designs, 20th century yarn rugs were made with a wide variety of techniques not related to knitting of earlier times.

Knit or Not Knit?

One of the problems with tracing the history of knitted rugs is that it's not always easy to tell what technique was used in antique rugs. For example, some needlepoint stitches look like knitting on the surface, and shaggy surfaces hide the construction of many pile rugs. Even for knitters, identifying techniques is problematic because we can't take precious antiques apart to examine their construction.

Some needlepoint stitches look just like knitting.
Photo courtesy of Valerie Justin

Reversible shirred pile rugs had snippets of rags strung onto the yarn like beads, and then slid up to the knitting between stitches.
Photo courtesy of Allen Arthur Cyber Rug Center

TODAY'S RENAISSANCE OF KNITTED RUGS

Today we are experiencing a renaissance of knitted rugs as artisan knitters are once again viewing the rug as a canvas for their creativity. Modern pieces reflect the full spectrum of historical techniques at the same time fiber artists explore new yarns and exciting designs.

Along with the expansion of artistry in knitted rugs comes the growing realization that knitted rugs are suitable for many uses—not only floor coverings, but also table covers, wall hangings, blankets, and yoga mats. Contemporary works range from practical home décor accessories to outlandish and thought-provoking tapestries. Each is a remarkable study in texture and color and a celebration of the creativity of today's textile artists. You'll see the work of contemporary rug artists below and on pages 16-17. Some were made by full-time professional rug designers, others were made by talented amateurs. These art works as well as the 21 everyday rug projects I've presented to demonstrate basic rug knitting techniques, all share the same simple beginnings—two needles, a ball of yarn, and a vision of making something beautiful and practical.

Jim Simpson, Australian bushman and WWII Air Force pilot, knit this modern masterpiece while in a German prison camp. Using yarn recycled from old sweaters and needles made of cooking pot handles, he designed this map of his beloved homeland from memory.
(Right, Jim Simpson; left, John Harpley)
Photo courtesy of Rob Willis

Carol Rasmussen Noble created a beautiful rug with simple Garter Stitch and subtle colors. Photo by Dominic Cotignola

gallery

This rug, made by *Linda Romens*, combines a modern-art style Intarsia design with more traditional mosaic borders. The collection of colors may inspire you to draw up your own chart on graph paper, and knit a rug using all of the leftover yarn from the projects you've made over the years.

Knit and purl stitches are combined in different combinations and knit it one piece in this handspun rug, Shades of Grey, by *Katharine Cobey.*

Henry the Cat, knit in black and white angora, by *Lucy Neatby*, shows how soft yarn and small designs are perfect for knitted pillows.

This brightly colored half-circle hearth rug by *Diana Blake Gray* is made from the cotton fabric normally used for quilting. The printed calico fabric turns into a variegated blend when you cut it into strips to "make your own" yarn.

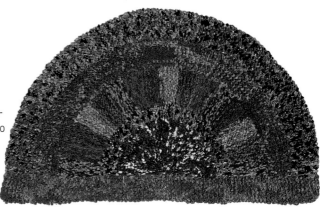

All Gallery photos are by Dominic Cotignola

This simple rug by *Rob Price* is a wonderful example of the beautiful projects that young children can knit. (Rob had a smidgen of help from his mother, Kathy Lenning-Sumpter.) Instead of making each color into a separate section as I did on the Knitted Cord Oval Runner, Rob and Kathy sewed their rug together as two intertwining spirals.

Made with handspun yarns in natural colors, *Katharine Cobey's* rug is an noteworthy example of mitered square knitting. Each square has stripes of different shade yarns, adding a bit of whimsy to the staid color palette.

The dance of colors in the handpainted yarns *Carol Rasmussen Noble* used to knit the Northern Lights Rug truly bring the colors of the Northern sky to life. The geometric Intarsia color work design in Garter Stitch shows off the texture of the yarn.

This Escher-esque fish by *Lucy Neatby* combines Intarsia and Fair Isle color knitting with many different texture stitches.

Made from T-shirt knit fabric by *Diana Blake Gray*, this circular rug with a pinwheel center combines traditional techniques with modern materials. The stretchy fabric is easier to knit than woven woolens or cotton, and it adds a contemporary flavor to this classic Garter Stitch design.

knitting basics

I can't remember a time when I did not know how to knit. On summer vacations when I was in grade school, my grandmother taught me how to knit and purl, cast on, and make honeycomb cables. Even though knitting is "just like riding a bike," I needed a refresher when I wanted to pick up the needles again 25 years later.

Whether you need a first lesson in knitting or a refresher, you'll find what you need in this chapter to get started.

○ In Before You Begin (page 19) you'll learn about knitting needles and tools, tips for selecting rug yarn, and different ways to hold the yarn and needles for knitting.

○ Getting Started with Garter Stitch (page 24) shows you how to get stitches onto the knitting needles and practice the basic knit stitch. After learning the basics, you'll be able to make any of the Garter Stitch projects.

Easy Garter Stitch rugs are good bets for beginning knitters.

○ Progressing to Purls (page 28) explains how to add the purl stitch and new cast-on and bind-off techniques to your knitting repertoire. After learning these new skills, you'll be ready to make rugs with different pattern stitches.

○ In Knitting from Patterns (page 30) you'll find tips on reading the pattern instructions, joining a new ball of yarn, measuring gauge, and fixing mistakes. This section also includes lists of the knitting abbreviations and chart symbols used in the rug pattern.

before you begin

To learn to knit, you need beginner's hands and a beginner's mind. Your beginner's mind will want to soak in all of the information and techniques at once. But it will take a lot longer for your beginner's hands to learn the motions of knitting than it does for your mind to understand the concepts. Don't worry if you are slow, if you make mistakes, or if you feel awkward. You'll get past this with practice.

After you learn to combine knits and purls, you can make rugs using different pattern stitches, such as this Coiled Cord Rug.

KNITTING TOOLS

To get started knitting, you need only a few basic tools, available from most yarn and craft stores:

☞ Knitting needles

☞ A knitting bag large enough to hold your project and with a pocket to hold small tools

☞ Zipper-locking freezer bags or plastic pencil pouches to help organize your tools and keep yarn clean and dry

☞ A small tape measure that fits in your knitting bag

☞ A blunt tapestry needle for weaving in ends and sewing seams

☞ Small scissors for trimming ends

☞ A photocopy of your pattern and a pencil so you can make notes as you go

Later, you'll want to add more things to your knitting bag:

☞ An emery board and hand cream to keep your fingers from catching on your knitting

☞ Crochet hooks for picking up dropped stitches and adding edgings

☞ Sticky notes for marking your place on charts

☞ A calculator

☞ Needle-point protectors, stitch markers, row counters, and plastic pins

☞ More knitting bags (eventually, you'll find yourself with more than one project "on the needles")

KNITTING NEEDLES

Knitting needles are the tools you'll use most often, so take the time to try different kinds and see what's most comfortable for you. Needles come in many shapes, sizes, and materials. Each type behaves differently. Here are some options to consider:

Circular, straight, or double-pointed. I use circular needles for large flat-knitting projects so I don't have to scrunch my knitting onto straight needles. I also find that circular needles put less stress on my wrists, since I carry the bulk of my knitting on the cable in my lap. For small projects and for knitting narrow strips, I use straight or double-pointed needles.

Size. Knitting needles come in different sizes, or thickness. In the US, sizes are numbered. In most other countries, needle size is measured in millimeters. A needle gauge tool has holes marked with various needle sizes, so you can measure needles that are not marked. Only large needle sizes are appropriate for knitting rugs.

Length. Needles come in different lengths. I find straight needles over 12 inches/30cm long cumbersome and heavy. But if your project pieces are wide, you may find working with the longer needles easier than scrunching your stitches onto shorter ones. I like circular needles slightly longer than my knitting is wide, so I can look at my knitting as I progress.

Metal, bamboo, wood, or plastic. For beginning knitters, wooden or bamboo needles are good choices. Smooth and comfortable, they are not as slippery as metal or plastic needles. Your knitting goes a little more slowly, but you won't drop as many stitches. After you've finished a few projects, try plastic or metal needles. These are faster than wood, but give slightly less control. Wood and plastic are warmer than metal needles, and you may find them more comfortable, especially in colder weather.

Metric (mm)	US
4.5	7
5	8
5.5	9
6	10
6.5-7	10½
8	11
9	13
10	15
12	17
15	19

about measurements

Some knitters insist that you get more accurate measurements with a soft tape measure because your knitting is also soft, while others claim that you get more accurate measurements with a yard stick. An inch is an inch is an inch, and whether it's printed on metal, plastic, or tape, 1 inch is always equal to 2.5cm. I use a small tape measure because it's convenient and I can carry it with me.

All the measurements in *The Knitted Rug*—except needle sizes—are given first in U.S. measurements, with the approximate metric measurement immediately after.

In accordance with the Craft Yarn Council guidelines, in an attempt to standardize knitting measurements across the globe, knitting needle measurements are first given in metric, then U.S. sizes.

Rug yarns today are so beautiful, even everyday rugs become works of art.

YARN

Knitted rugs are made with *yarn* or *fabric strips*. I made all of the projects in this book with yarn because so many beautiful choices are available today. (If you want to try using fabric strips to knit rugs, see Rag Rugs on page 23.) Each pattern includes information for using a specific yarn, plus suggestions for substituting other yarns in case the recommended yarn is no longer available or you want to personalize the design.

YARN FIBERS

The selection in your local yarn shop can be exhilarating. Each type of yarn has different properties, benefits, and drawbacks. The materials you choose should be based on how you intend to use your rug and the style of your décor.

Protein fibers are easy to knit because they have natural give, or stretch. These include wool, alpaca, mohair, and silk. Depending on the type of animal and specific breed, yarns from animal fibers can be soft enough to wear next to a baby's skin or strong enough to wipe your feet on.

Cellulose fibers usually have less give than protein fibers and often make stronger yarns. Some are even used to make ropes. These include cotton, linen, and hemp. Mercerized cotton yarn is lustrous and drapes well, while unmercerized cotton is more absorbent and softer. Cotton fabric is the favorite for quilting and for good reason. It's both soft and durable. Hemp and linen are usually coarser and stronger than cotton.

Synthetics are man-made fibers, generally made from petroleum derivatives. These fibers, including nylon, polyester, and acrylic, can be machine-washed and dried, and make practical, hardwearing items. Acrylic yarns sometimes pill more than other yarns.

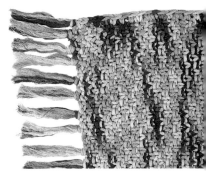

Basketweave Felted Runner is made from wool, a protein fiber.

Country Kitchen Moss Stitch Rug is made from cotton, a cellulose fiber.

Knit-and-Sew Washboard Runner is made with blends of wool and acrylic.

The Chenille rug from the Quick-Knit Garter Stitch Trio is made with a novelty yarn.

Blends are yarns that combine the characteristics of two or more fibers.

Novelty yarns are usually produced from man-made fibers or several different fibers blended or plied together in unusual textures and color combinations.

SINGLES AND PLIED YARNS

Yarn is made by twisting, or *spinning*, fibers together into a long strand. Yarn made from one strand is called a *single*. Singles are sometimes twisted together into yarns called *two-ply*, *three-ply*, and so on. In smooth knitting yarns, all of the strands are the same fiber or blend, and the same thickness. In novelty yarns, strands of different fibers, textures, and thickness are often combined.

BALLS AND SKEINS

Yarn is put up in balls, pull-skeins, cones, or hanks. You can work directly from a cone, ball, or pull-skein, but hanks will tangle if you try to knit without first making a ball.

Most yarn stores have a swift and ball-winder and will often do this for you. Here's how to make a ball of yarn without tools:

1. Open the skein, being careful not to tangle, and place it over the back of a chair.

2. Wind the yarn loosely in a ball, wrapping it around your fingers to keep the yarn from stretching too tightly.

Rugs are usually knit from the three heaviest weights of yarn: 4 Medium, 5 Bulky, and 6 Super Bulky.

YARN WEIGHTS

Yarns come in many weights from fine, almost threadlike lace weight to heavy, ropelike super bulky. Only heavy yarns are appropriate for knitting rugs. While the names of the different weights may seem strange, each weight knits up to a recommended *gauge* (number of stitches per inch or cm) on a suggested needle size.

Note: You may need to use a different needle size to "get gauge." See page 30 for tips on knitting and measuring a gauge swatch.

If you're not sure what you need, check the yarn label for gauge and needle size recommendations.

Weight	Description	Gauge (per inch/2.5cm)	Metric Needle Size	U.S. Needle Size
4 Medium	Worsted, afghan, or Aran weight yarn	4-5 sts	4.5-5.5mm	7-9
5 Bulky	Chunky, craft, or rug yarn	3-4 sts	5.5-8mm	9-11
6 Super Bulky	Bulky yarn or roving	1½ to 2-2½ sts	8mm and larger	11 and larger

COLOR AND DYE LOT

Yarns are dyed in batches called *dye lots*. The dye lot is indicated by a number on the yarn label. Make sure you check the labels, and buy enough of the same dye lot to complete your project. Even if skeins from different dye lots look the same on the shelf in the yarn shop, the subtle color difference may be distracting in the finished rug. Buying an extra ball or two "just in case" is a good idea. Most yarn shops will gladly let you return or exchange leftover balls. Check with your local yarn shop about their specific return policy when purchasing your yarn.

Some synthetic yarns are dyed with a new process called "no dye lot"—the colors match, and variations, if any, are slight.

Photo courtesy La Lana Wools, Taos, New Mexico

Hand-painted and variegated yarns have several colors combined in one skein to create multicolored designs as you knit. These yarns also have dye lots. Hand-painted yarns may have subtle differences even when the skeins come from the same dye lot. To avoid sharp changes in color when changing skeins, use two different balls of yarn at the same time. Work two rows from one skein, then two rows from the other.

rag rugs

Did you know you can make your own yarn from fabric strips? Several projects in this book include tips on using your own homemade yarn. Most fabrics will work, but don't mix fabrics from different fibers because they won't shrink or wear evenly.

☞ Cut strips ½ to 1¼"/1 to 3cm wide (narrower for heavy fabric, wider for lightweight fabric). Fold wider strips in half lengthwise to form a bulky strand, or double fold to hide the raw edges.

☞ For strong strips, snip the fabric near the edge, then cut or tear straight across, as in figure 1.

☞ For flexible strips, use a rotary cutter to cut on the bias (diagonally), as in figure 2.

☞ To avoid seams, cut fabric in continuous strips. Figures 3 and 4 show two different ways to cut them.

To use fabric as pile, cut strips into lengths of 2 or 3"/5 or 7.5cm.

To use fabric as knitting yarn, knot or sew strips to form a long strand, and wind into a ball.

☞ When *knotting* strips use a square knot or overhand knot. The knots will disappear in between the garter ridges.

☞ When *sewing* fabric cut the ends diagonally, and overlap 2"/5cm, as in figure 5. Stitch along both long edges.

Use special lacing thread or heavy string to seam, or *lace*, the pieces of rag rugs together with invisible seams or whipstitch. As you sew, make sure the rug is flat. Fabric strips don't block to shape easily.

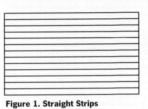

Figure 1. Straight Strips

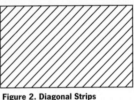

Figure 2. Diagonal Strips

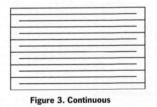

Figure 3. Continuous Strips #1

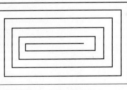

Figure 4. Continuous Strips #2

Figure 5. How to Sew Fabric Strips as Knitting Yarn

The brown yarn is made from fleece, a modern material. Cotton strips, used in the green yarn, will make a lovely old-fashioned rug.

HOLDING THE YARN AND NEEDLES

There are many ways to hold the yarn and needles in knitting, but the *English* and *Continental* methods are most common. In both methods, you hold both needles loosely under your palms, secured between your thumb and fingers. Leave your index fingers free for managing the yarn.

If you are a new knitter, you may want to try both methods to see which is most comfortable for you.

HOLDING THE YARN IN YOUR RIGHT HAND—ENGLISH METHOD

In the English, or American, method, you hold the working yarn (the yarn attached to the ball) with your *right hand*. This is the most common method of knitting in the United States.

1. To control the tension of the yarn, wrap the working yarn around your little finger and over your index finger (see figure 1).

2. Then grasp the needle between your thumb and fingers (see figure 2).

English
HOLDING THE YARN

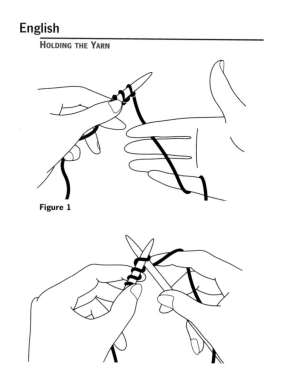

Figure 1

Figure 2

HOLDING THE YARN IN YOUR LEFT HAND—CONTINENTAL METHOD

In the Continental, or German, method, you hold the working yarn (the yarn attached to the ball) with your *left hand*. This is my favorite knitting method because I learned to knit this way from my grandmother. This method may also be easier for lefties and crocheters.

1. To control the tension, wrap the yarn around your right index finger several times. Drop a wrap from your finger whenever you need more yarn to complete a stitch (see figure 1).

2. Another way to tension the yarn is to wrap the working yarn around your little finger, and then hold it with your index finger (see figure 2).

Continental
HOLDING THE YARN

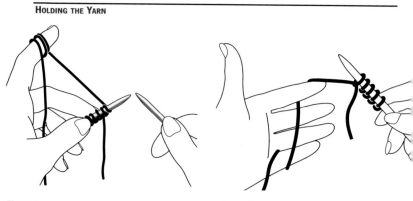

Figure 1   **Figure 2**

getting started with garter stitch

The pattern stitch made by knitting every stitch in every row is *Garter Stitch*. This is the first basic pattern stitch in knitting, and the easiest to knit. Garter Stitch lies perfectly flat and is thicker than most other knitting pattern stitches, making it an excellent choice for rugs.

To get started, you'll need a pair of 5.5-8mm (size 9-11 U.S.) knitting needles and a ball of bulky yarn. Most rugs are knit on the larger needles, but if you've never knit before, you might find it easier to practice with needles on the smaller end of the scale.

THE LONG TAIL CAST ON

To start knitting, you first place a foundation row of stitches on the needle. This is called casting on. The long tail cast on is the most common method. It creates a flexible edge that is appropriate for almost any project.

To get started, pull out a "long tail" of yarn about four times the width of the rug you are making. For practice, leave a 48"/122cm tail. Make a slipknot and put it on the needle. This is the first stitch.

LONG TAIL CAST ON—ENGLISH METHOD

1. With the needle in your right hand, wind the loose end of the yarn around your left thumb as shown in figure 1.

2. Insert the needle into the loop on your thumb, from bottom to top, as in figure 2.

3. With your right index finger, wrap the working yarn around the needle. Pull the yarn back through the loop on your thumb from top to bottom. Then pull your thumb out of the loop. (See figure 3.) You now have another stitch on the needle.

4. Repeat steps 1 to 3 until you have the required stitches on the right needle. For practice, cast on 20 stitches.

LONG TAIL CAST ON—CONTINENTAL METHOD

1. With the tail of the yarn over your left thumb and the yarn attached to the ball over your index finger, pull the strands open. Grasp the strands in your palm, and pull the needle down to form a "V" between your thumb and index finger (see figure 1).

2. Insert the needle into the loop on your thumb, from bottom to top (see figure 2). Bring the needle around the yarn on your index finger from right to left, and catch the yarn on the needle. Then pull the yarn back through the loop on your thumb from top to bottom.

3. Pull your thumb out of the loop. You now have another stitch on the needle. Reposition your thumb under the tail, and tug gently to tighten the new stitch on the needle (see figure 3). Do not let go of the strands held in your palm.

4. Repeat steps 2 and 3 until you have the required stitches on the right needle. For practice, cast on 20 stitches.

How to Make a Slipknot
A slipknot attaches the working yarn to your knitting needles. If you've never made one before, here's how:

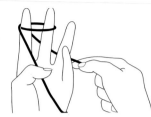

1. Make a loop in the yarn.

2. Pull the working yarn through the loop, creating a new loop.

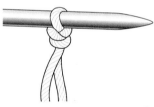

3. Put the new loop on the needle, and tug on the ends to tighten.

English
LONG TAIL CAST

![Figure 1]
Figure 1

![Figure 2]
Figure 2

![Figure 3]
Figure 3

Continental
LONG TAIL CAST

![Figure 1]
Figure 1

![Figure 2]
Figure 2

![Figure 3]
Figure 3

Tip

If you get frustrated learning to cast on, ask an experienced knitter to cast on for your first project. Once you practice knitting and get comfortable holding the yarn and needles, casting on will be easier.

Tip

If you notice that you're casting on tightly, cast on with a needle one or two sizes larger than you use to knit the rest of the project.

THE KNIT STITCH

Now that you have stitches on a needle, you can begin knitting.

Note: If you have trouble getting started with your knitting, don't panic. The first row is always the hardest, especially if your cast on is tight.

Note: Don't knit on the tips of the needles. Your stitches will be too tight and you may have trouble knitting the next row.

KNIT STITCH—ENGLISH METHOD

1. Hold the needle with the stitches in your left hand and the empty needle in your right hand. With the working yarn in back of the needle, insert the right needle under the left needle and into the first stitch from front to back (see figure 1).

2. With your right index finger, wrap the working yarn around the right needle counterclockwise (see figure 2).

Note: When you first try this, you may find that you let go of the right needle while you're wrapping the yarn. This is okay, but it's slow. To speed up your knitting, keep your hand on the right needle, and stretch out your index finger to throw the yarn around the needle.

3. Pull the yarn through the loop on the left needle (see figure 3).

4. Drop the old stitch from the left needle. You now have one new stitch on the right needle (see figure 4). Repeat the steps to knit across the row until all of the stitches are on the right needle.

KNIT STITCH—CONTINENTAL METHOD

1. Hold the needle with the stitches in your left hand and the empty needle in your right hand. With the working yarn in back of the left needle, insert the right needle under the left needle and into the first stitch from front to back (see figure 1).

2. Move the tip of the right needle behind the working yarn from right to left, then bring it to the front again to catch the yarn (see figure 2).

3. Pull the yarn through the loop on the left needle (see figure 3).

4. Drop the old stitch from the left needle. You now have one new stitch on the right needle (see figure 4). Repeat the steps to knit across the row until all of the stitches are on the right needle.

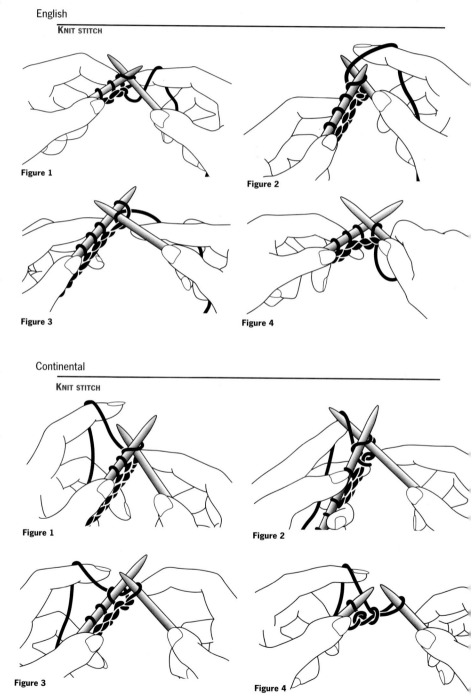

English

KNIT STITCH

Figure 1

Figure 2

Figure 3

Figure 4

Continental

KNIT STITCH

Figure 1

Figure 2

Figure 3

Figure 4

THE DECREASE BIND OFF

When you're finished knitting, you need to bind off the last row of stitches.

The decrease bind off is worked two stitches at a time, with each stitch being put back on the left needle after it is knit. Make sure to work the bind off row loosely. Use larger needles if necessary.

1. Knit two stitches together through the back loops: insert the needle through two loops on the left-hand needle at once, and work them together as in figure 1.

2. Move the stitch on the right needle back onto the left needle, as in figure 2.

3. Repeat steps 1 and 2 until there is only one loop left on the needle.

Cut the working yarn from the ball, leaving a few inches for weaving in. Take the last loop off the needle, and pull the new tail through the loop. Give it a little tug to tighten.

Congratulations! You're ready to start your first project. See the Easy Garter Stitch projects, beginning on page 57 for a selection of beginner projects.

Note: If you've never worked from a knitting pattern before, take a quick look at Knitting from Patterns on page 30 for some tips that will make your project go smoothly.

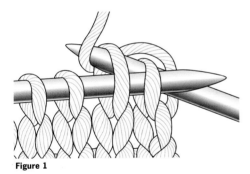

Figure 1

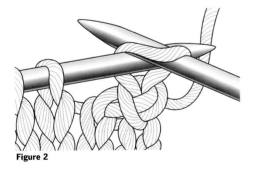

Figure 2

making a garter stitch swatch

A swatch is a sample of knitting that is used to practice new pattern stitches and to test what size needle you'll use to make your knitting come out the right size.

Note: Right now don't worry about the size, or gauge, of your swatch. But if you're curious, see Measuring a Gauge Swatch on page 31 for more technical information.

To begin a new row, you must "turn your work." Flip the right needle around and switch hands so it becomes the left needle. Use the empty needle as the right needle. For practice, knit 40 rows to create a swatch.

Note: Make sure to bring the working yarn under the needle to the back as you start each new row. If you bring the yarn over the needle to the back, you may accidentally add an extra stitch.

As you knit your practice swatch, you may notice that both sides of Garter Stitch look the same. To keep track of the right side, attach a safety pin or a piece of scrap yarn to the front of your work. Unless a pattern specifies differently, the first row you knit is the right side.

The terms "right side" and "wrong side" are usually abbreviated as RS and WS in knitting instructions. The right side is the front of the rug, the wrong side is the back. For a list of other knitting abbreviations that I've used in this book, see page 32.

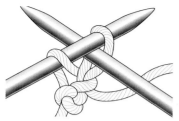

Figure 1

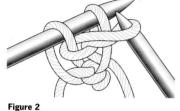

Figure 2

Figure 3

progressing to purls

There are only two stitches in knitting—the knit and the purl. These two stitches can be combined in infinite combinations of color, texture, and pattern. Now that you've learned and practiced the knit stitch, it's time to progress to purling.

THE CABLE CAST ON

The cable cast on technique uses two needles and is similar to creating a row of knitting. It creates a beaded border that looks nice with knit-and-purl pattern stitches and makes a stable edge for rugs. My favorite feature of the cable cast on is that you don't have to measure out a long tail.

1. Make a slipknot about 4"/10cm from the end of the yarn (see slipknot instructions on page 25). This is the first stitch.

2. Knit one stitch. Leave the slipknot on the left needle, and place the new stitch back on the left needle as well. You now have two stitches on the left needle and the right needle is empty.

3. Insert the right needle between the last two stitches on the left needle and wrap the yarn as if to knit. (See figure 1.)

4. Pull the yarn through. (See figure 2.)

Note: When working with rug yarns, pull through a loop about 1"/2.5cm long. Don't worry about making the cast on stitches too loose. That's almost impossible.

5. Place the new stitch back on the left needle as shown in figure 3.

Don't tighten the new stitch until after you insert the needle between the two stitches.

6. Repeat steps 3 through 5 for the required number of stitches. For practice, cast on 20 stitches. Then knit one row. This is the right side (RS).

THE PURL STITCH

The purl stitch is the second basic stitch in knitting. It's similar to the knit stitch, but is made with the working yarn in front of the needles.

PURL STITCH—ENGLISH METHOD

1. With the working yarn in front of the left needle, insert the right needle into the first stitch from back to front, as in figure 1.

2. Wrap the working yarn around the right needle counterclockwise, as in figure 2.

3. Pull the yarn through, as in figure 3.

4. Drop the old stitch from the left needle. (See figure 4.) You now have one new stitch on the right needle. Repeat these steps to purl across the row until all of the stitches are on the right needle.

English

PURL STITCH

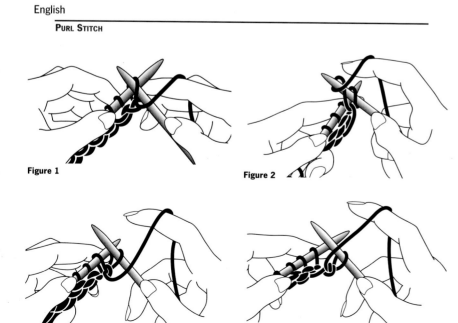

Figure 1

Figure 2

Figure 3

Figure 4

PURL STITCH—CONTINENTAL METHOD

1. With the working yarn in front of the needle, insert the right needle into the first stitch from back to front, as in figure 1.

2. Wrap the working yarn around the right needle counterclockwise. Use your left index finger to pull the yarn down behind the right needle, as in figure 2.

3. Pull the yarn through, as in figure 3.

4. Drop the old stitch from the left needle. (See figure 4.) You now have one new stitch on the right needle. Repeat these steps to purl across the row until all of the stitches are on the right needle.

IN PATTERN BIND OFF

This bind off is worked as a regular row, with each stitch being eliminated after it is worked. The advantage to this technique is that you can bind off "in pattern"—that is, you can either knit or purl each stitch before eliminating it.

Because your swatch is Stockinette Stitch and you're binding off on a RS row, bind off all stitches knitwise, that is, knit each stitch before eliminating it.

1. Starting on a RS row, knit one stitch.

2. Knit another stitch. You now have two stitches on the right needle.

3. Insert the left needle into the second stitch on the right needle as in figure 1 below, (instructions continue on page 30).

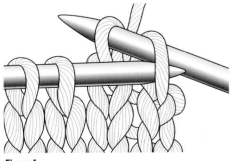
Figure 1

Continental

PURL STITCH

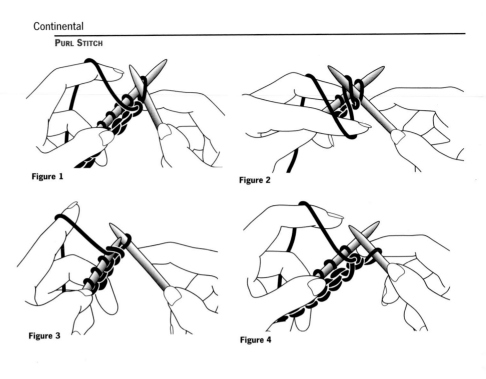

Figure 1

Figure 2

Figure 3

Figure 4

making a stockinette stitch swatch

The second basic knitted fabric is Stockinette Stitch. When working back and forth, this is created by knitting every stitch on the right side (RS) rows and purling every stitch on the wrong side (WS) rows. For practice, work 30 rows in Stockinette Stitch, ending with a WS row.

Keeping track of the right side is easy with Stockinette Stitch. Each stitch looks like a little V on the knit side, and like a "bump" on the purl side. (See how purling is like "knitting inside out"—all of the stitches look like "V"s on the front of the knitted fabric and bumps on the back-there's no way to tell which row was knitted and which was purled.) You may notice that even though your Stockinette Stitch swatch has fewer rows than your Garter Stitch swatch, it's taller. The Stockinette Stitch swatch is also narrower than the Garter Stitch swatch, even though you cast on 20 stitches for both swatches. This is because each pattern stitch works up to a different gauge. (See Measuring a Gauge Swatch on page 31 to learn more about gauge.)

Stockinette Stitch and Reverse Stockinette Stitch are both made by knitting and purling alternate rows. The only difference is which side is chosen as the right side. With Stockinette Stitch, the Vs are the right side; with Reverse Stockinette, the purl bumps are the right side.

When you're using a combination of knits and purls in a pattern stitch, your pattern may tell you to "knit the knits and purl the purls." This means when you come to a V on your knitting, you knit a stitch, when you come to a bump, you purl.

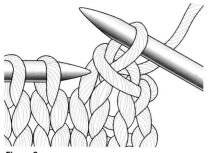

Figure 2

4. Pass it over the first, dropping it off the needles. One stitch remains on the right needle as in figure 2.

5. Repeat steps 2 to 4 until you have bound off all stitches.

Note: Stockinette Stitch curls at the edges, as you may notice on your swatch. Adding a border of Garter Stitch, Seed Stitch, single crochet, or fringe will make the rug lie flat. I used this technique in the Waterfall Fringe (page 95) and Knit-and-Purl Hearth (page 77) rugs.

Note: You can also combine knit and purl stitches in other combinations, or pattern stitches, such as the ones I used in the Country Kitchen Moss Stitch Rug (page 80) and the Hemp Doormat (page 84).

the project go smoothly, collect everything on the list before you start.

Gauge. This section tells you how many stitches and rows are in 4"/10cm of the rug. Even if you don't care about the exact size of the finished rug, making a gauge swatch is important. Here are some questions to ask:

☞ Is the fabric texture and firmness appropriate for the intended use of the rug?

☞ Is it strong enough to take wear on the floor?

☞ Is it too stretchy to hang on the wall?

☞ Is it soft enough for an exercise mat or bed rug?

☞ Did you enjoy knitting this swatch? If your knitting is too tight, you may find it difficult to knit, especially on the first few rows. If your knitting is too loose, your fabric will look sloppy, and it's easier to make mistakes such as dropping stitches.

knitting from patterns

Before you begin a new project, read the instructions carefully, and make sure you understand all of the steps and techniques that are used. The patterns in this book include the sections listed below.

Skill Level. Knitting projects are categorized into one of four experience levels—from beginner to experienced—to show what skills are required to complete the project. Whatever your skill level, you'll find projects in this book that will be just right for you.

Finished Measurements. This section tells you the finished size of the rug in the photograph. Your rug will be the same size if you get the same gauge and follow the instructions exactly. However, you may intentionally choose to alter the size of the rug. On those projects where this is easy to do, I've included tips on resizing.

Materials. This lists the type and amount of yarn, size and type of knitting needles, and other tools, such as row counters or darning needles that you'll need to complete the project. To make

Tip

Don't worry too much about the skill level designations. If you're up for a challenge, and you can understand the instructions after reading them over once or twice, go ahead and try something that will stretch your skills.

Skill level	Description
Beginner	These are ideal first projects for new knitters.
Easy	These projects are made with basic stitches and have simple shaping and finishing.
Intermediate	These projects have more challenging stitches and finishing techniques.
Experienced	These projects are for knitters with experience, who are ready for advanced techniques and complicated stitch patterns.

Pattern Stitches. Instructions for any special pattern stitches—combinations of knits and purls—are given here.

Charts and Diagrams. Some pattern stitches and rug shapes are easier to show with a picture than to explain in text. In some projects, I've included charts or diagrams to show you how to knit color designs, cables, and unusual shapes. (See Knitting Symbols and Charts on page 32 for information on how to read charts.)

Instructions. This section includes step-by-step instructions for completing the rug.

Finishing. Information on embellishing, backing, and blocking your rug are in this section.

Historical Techniques and Rag Rug Techniques. These two sections include hard-to-find information on how to adapt historical techniques to your rugs.

Design Tips. This is where I've included ideas for customizing the rug to match the décor of your home

measuring a gauge swatch

Gauge is a measurement of how tight your knitting is. It is measured in stitches per inch or cm (width) and rows per inch or cm (height).

Making a gauge swatch is easy. Using the stitch pattern and needles recommended for the project, cast on about 20 to 24 stitches, and work until you have about 5"/13cm of knitting. If the instructions say the gauge is measured after blocking, steam or wash your swatch according to the finishing instructions for the project.

Stitch gauge is important in almost all projects. If your stitch gauge is not exact, your rug will not come out the width indicated in the pattern. To measure the stitch gauge, place a ruler or tape measure across your swatch horizontally. Mark the beginning and end of 4"/10cm, and count the stitches.

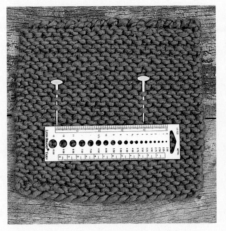

To measure stitch gauge on Garter Stitch, count the bumps on the top of the row.

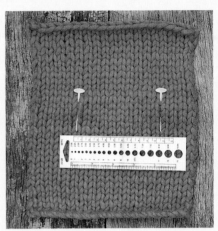

To measure stitch gauge on Stockinette Stitch, count the Vs.

Row gauge is less important for rugs because they have little shaping and you can knit to the desired length without counting rows on most projects. To measure the row gauge, place a ruler or tape measure vertically across your swatch. Mark the beginning and end of 4"/10cm with pins or masking tape. Count the rows according to the type of stitch as in the figures below.

Note: If the number of stitches and rows in your swatch are:

☛ more than recommended, try again with a larger needle

☛ fewer than recommended, try a smaller needle.

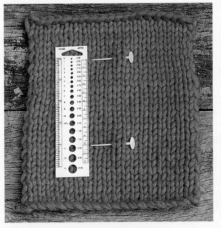

To measure row gauge on Stockinette Stitch, count the Vs.

To measure row gauge on Garter Stitch, count the ridges and multiply by 2. Two rows make one ridge.

KNITTING ABBREVIATIONS

Knitting patterns are often full of abbreviations intended to save space. I have used some abbreviations in the pattern instructions, but have tried to keep them to a minimum.

Term	Definition
cm	centimeter
cn	cable needle
dec	decrease
dpn	double-pointed needles
inc	increase
k or K	knit
k2tog	knit 2 together
m1	make one
p or P	purl
pm	place marker
RS	right side
rnd	round
ssk	slip 1, slip1, knit
sl	slip
st(s)	stitch(es)
St st	stockinette stitch, stocking stitch
wyif	with yarn in front
wyib	with yarn in back
WS	wrong side

KNITTING SYMBOLS AND CHARTS

Sometimes stitch patterns have both charts and written instructions.

A chart is a picture of the stitch pattern made using special symbols (for pattern stitches) or squares of colors (for color work). Each square in the chart represents one stitch. The symbols are a shorthand for those knitters who learn more easily from visual information. Page 33 has two examples of knitting charts.

Symbol	Definition
▯	knit on RS, purl on WS
▬	knit on WS, purl on RS
⌀	m1
◿	k2tog
◺	ssk
▨	no stitch
	4-st right cable
	4-st left cable
	4-st right purl cable
	4-st left purl cable
	6-st right cable
	6-st left cable

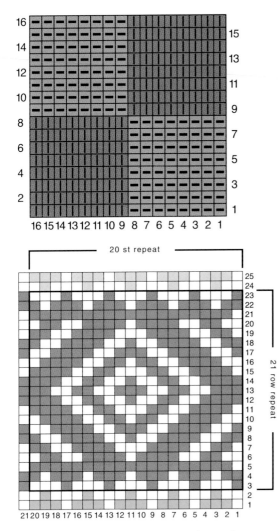

20 st repeat

21 row repeat

To read a chart, start at the bottom for row 1.

☞ If you're knitting back and forth, RS rows are read from right to left. WS rows are read from left to right.

☞ If you're knitting in the round: all rows are read from right to left.

Note: Charts for Mosaic knitting are read differently from other knitting charts. Each row on the chart represents two rows of knitting. See page 40 in Special Techniques for instructions on working from mosaic charts.

Charts for pattern stitches frequently are accompanied by written instructions. These are helpful if you're not familiar with the symbols used in the chart, or if you're more comfortable learning from instructions.

JOINING A NEW BALL OF YARN

When you make a large project, you'll most likely need more than one ball of yarn. If you come across a knot in the yarn, untie it, or cut the knot apart, and follow the same instructions for joining a new ball.

If you're working in stripes, or if the edge of the rug will be enclosed in a crochet border or covered by a fringe, start the new ball at the beginning of the row: (See figure 1.)

1. At the end of the row, leave a tail 5"/12.5cm long on the old yarn.

2. Tie the new yarn onto the old yarn with an overhand knot near the edge of the fabric leaving a tail on this yarn as well. See figure 1.

3. Start knitting with the new yarn. You need a tail of yarn at least four times the width of the rug plus 5"/12.5cm to work one complete row and change yarns at the end of the row. If in doubt, change yarns so you don't run out in the middle of a row.

If the edge of your rug will not be embellished, you can start the new ball in the middle of the row so you don't break up the smooth selvage. (See figure 2.)

1. When a tail 5"/12.5cm long remains on the old yarn, start knitting with the new yarn, also leaving a tail that is 5"/12.5cm long.

2. Tie the two ends loosely on the wrong side of the work and keep going as in figure 2.

When you finish knitting the rug, untie the knots and weave in the tails. (For instructions on weaving in ends, see Finishing Touches on page 49.)

Figure 1

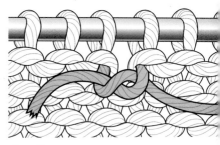

Figure 2

FIXING MISTAKES

If you make a mistake, don't panic or get discouraged. All knitters make mistakes. Even those of us with lots of experience still mess up now and again. Most problems can be fixed quickly and easily with a little help. Sometimes you can't fix a problem. But that doesn't mean your project is ruined. You'll have to rip out your knitting back to the point where everything is okay. If you get stuck, don't be afraid to ask a friend or local yarn shop owner to lend a hand.

With the skills you've learned in this chapter, you are ready to start making rugs. Use the next three chapters as you need them to look up the special techniques, finishing, and embellishment instructions used in the rug you're making.

Once you learn special techniques, such as those in the Fair Isle In-the-Round rug, you can apply them to other projects.

special techniques

In this chapter you'll find instructions for special techniques used in making the more advanced rugs in the book. Don't worry about learning these all at once. Each pattern includes the page numbers to refer you to the necessary techniques in this chapter, so all you have to do is flip back to this section when you need to.

TECHNIQUES USED IN EASY GARTER STITCH RUGS

These techniques are used in some of the Garter Stitch projects (beginning on page 57), as well as many of the other projects in the book.

INCREASES AND DECREASES

There are many ways to increase (add stitches) and decrease (remove stitches) from your knitting to shape pieces. Here a few easy methods. If you have another favorite method, feel free to substitute it in the projects.

The make one (M1) increase adds one stitch to your knitting.

1. With the tip of the left needle, lift the strand between the last stitch worked and the next stitch on the needle as in figure 1.

2. Knit into the back of the newly created loop to "make one" stitch.

The knit two together (K2tog) decrease removes one stitch from your knitting. This decrease slants to the right.

1. Insert the needle through two loops on the left needle at once, and work them together as a regular knit stitch as in figure 2.

Note: Sometimes you'll need to decrease on the WS. To purl two together (p2tog), insert the needle through two loops on the left needle at once as if to purl, and work them together as a regular purl stitch.

To make a mirror-image decrease that slants to the left, use a slip-slip-knit (ssk) decrease.

1. Slip the next two stitches one at a time to the right needle as if to knit.

2. Insert the left needle into the front of the stitches, and knit the two stitches together through the back loops with the right needle, as in figure 3.

The slip two, knit one, pass slipped stitches over (sl2, k1, p2sso) double decrease removes two stitches from your knitting at one time.

1. Sl2: Insert the right needle as if to knit through two loops on the left needle at once, and slip both stitches to the right needle, as in figure 4.

2. K1: Knit one stitch normally.

3. P2sso: Insert the left needle into the two slipped stitches on the right needle, and pass them over the knitted stitch, dropping them off the needles, as in figure 5. (If you have trouble passing both slipped stitches over at once, do them one at a time.)

SLIPPING STITCHES

When you "slip" a stitch, you move the stitch from the left needle to the right needle without knitting or purling. If the instructions say:

☞ Slip the stitch "as if to knit", insert the right needle into the next stitch on the left needle from front to back, as if you were going to knit, then slip the stitch onto the right needle without knitting it.

☞ Slip the stich "as if to purl", insert the right needle into the next stitch on the left needle from back to front, as if you were going to purl, then slip the stitch onto the right needle without purling it.

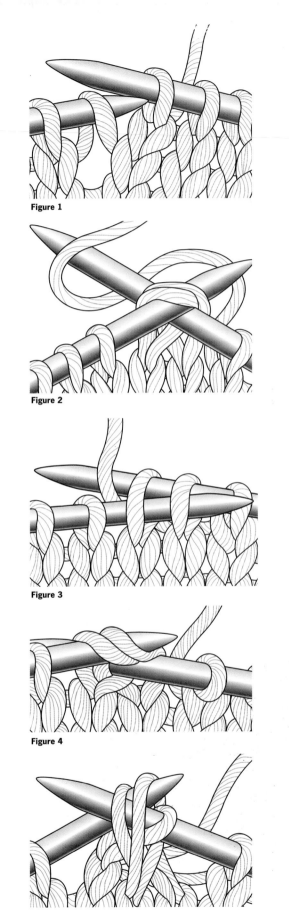

Figure 1

Figure 2

Figure 3

Figure 4

Figure 5

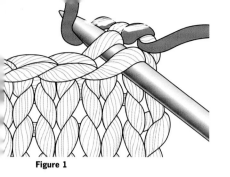

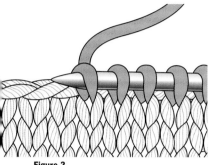

Figure 1

Figure 2

PICKING UP STITCHES

Sometimes knitted pieces are sewn together; at other times a new piece is knitted onto an existing piece. To attach a new section of knitting to an existing piece, you must pick up stitches along the edge of your knitting.

1. Insert the needle into the center of the stitch just inside the edge of your knitting, as in figure 1.

2. Pull the yarn through. You have picked up one stitch.

3. Repeat these steps to pick up the required number of stitches, as in figure 2.

To pick up stitches along the selvage (vertical edge) of Garter Stitch, insert the needle into the bumps at the end of the ridges.

When knitting patterns tell you to "pick up and knit" stitches, they actually mean to "pick up stitches as if to knit":

☛ In most cases you work with the right side facing, and you pick up and knit the new stitches. With the right side facing, insert the needle from front to back, and pull the yarn through to the front.

☛ Occasionally a pattern will tell you to pick up and purl the new stitches. With the wrong side facing, insert the needle from the back of the work to the front, wrap the yarn as if to purl, and pull it through to the back.

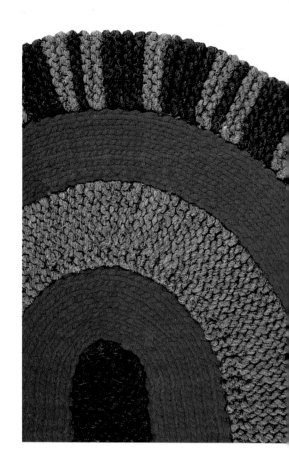

TECHNIQUES USED IN KNIT-AND-PURL RUGS

In addition to the pattern stitches used in the Knit-and-Purl rugs beginning on page 75, I also used short row shaping to curve the Stockinette stitch strips in the Knit-and-Purl Oval rug from this section.

SHORT ROW SHAPING

A short row is simply a row that has fewer stitches than the full piece of knitting. By knitting short rows along one side of a narrow knitted piece, you can make the piece curve.

Turning in the middle of the row leaves a small hole. The hole can be eliminated by wrapping the stitch at the turning point.

When instructions tell you to "wrap-and-turn":

1. Work to the turning point.

2. Wrap as in figure 1:

☛ Slip the next stitch onto the right needle.

☛ Bring the yarn to the front, then slip the same stitch back to the left needle.

3. Turn the work and knit or purl the next stitch. This wrap-and-turn technique creates a float (a piece of yarn that goes crossways on the face of the fabric, making a little bump) on the right side of the work.

On the next complete row, you will work back over the wrapped stitch. Knit the wrap together with the corresponding stitch on the left-hand needle to close up the holes created by the short row shaping (see figure 2).

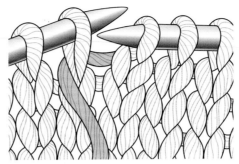

Figure 1

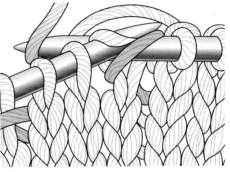

Figure 2

TECHNIQUES USED IN KNITTING PILE RUGS

Pile is made from short cut pieces of yarn put in between stitches to make a furry surface, or shag. Pile rugs (beginning on page 87) use basic knitting stitches combined with a few techniques to add the shaggy pile to the surface.

KNIT-IN PILE

You use two different types of yarn in pile knitting:

☛ Use a strong, medium-weight yarn, such as cotton or hemp, for knitting. This creates a background fabric for your rug.

☛ Use a plush, medium or bulky-weight yarn, such as wool or a novelty yarn, to make the pile (or shag).

To add strands of pile to Garter Stitch knitting, first cut the yarn that you'll use for the shag into 3"/7.5cm strips and set them aside. You'll use four pieces of medium-weight yarn or two pieces of bulky-weight yarn in each stitch. (Instructions are continued on page 38.)

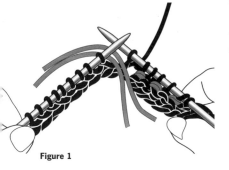

Figure 1

1. Knit one row plain. This is the RS.

2. The pile pieces are inserted between knitting stitches on WS rows.

☞ Knit one stitch, then insert 2 to 4 strands of pile yarn next to the stitch so half the strand is in front of the knitting and half is in back. (see figure 1.)

☞ Knit another stitch, then fold the pile strands over the new stitch so both ends of the pile are on the right side, which is at the back of your knitting.

3. Repeat steps 1 and 2, knitting all RS rows plain and inserting pile between stitches on WS rows. End on a row of plain knitting to lock in the last row of pile.

LOOPY PILE

Loopy pile is made with loops on the surface of the knitting. The loopy pile stitch is worked on a background of Garter Stitch. As you get started, you may feel clumsy trying to make the loops, but after a bit of practice you'll develop your own rhythm.

1. Knit one row plain. This is the RS.

2. Loops are made on WS rows. The loops are offset on every other WS row to make a more evenly spaced pile and to keep the loops from lining up in visible columns.

☞ On row 2, knit one stitch plain, then make a loop stitch. Repeat across the row, alternating between a plain stitch and a loop stitch.

☞ On row 4, you start with a loop, then knit a plain stitch.

Repeat steps 1 and 2, knitting plain on all RS rows and alternating between rows 2 and 4 for WS rows to create a loopy surface.

3. Now you're ready to make a finger loop. With the working yarn in back, insert the right needle into the next stitch as if to knit.

4. You can make the loop in either the English or Continental method.

English method: Put your left index finger behind the right needle, and wrap the yarn clockwise around the needle and your finger together and back across the needle a second time, as in figure 1.

English
LOOP

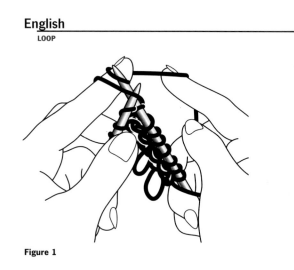

Figure 1

Continental method: With your left hand, wrap the working yarn counterclockwise around the needle and your right index finger, and back under the needle a second time, as in figure 2.

Continental
LOOP

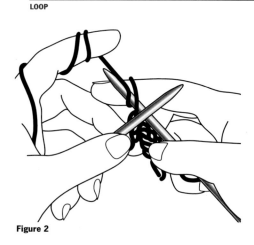

Figure 2

5. Use the right needle to draw the loops through, and drop the original stitch from the left needle.

6. Put the new loops back on the left needle, and knit into the back of these loops to lock the stitch in place.

Note: Keeping your index finger in the loop until after it is locked will help make all of your loops the same size.

TECHNIQUES USED IN COLOR-WORK RUGS

This section includes several different techniques for color knitting that are used on projects in the section on Color-Work rugs, beginning on page 99.

FAIR ISLE TWO-COLOR KNITTING

Knitting with two colors in a row to form color patterns that reach all the way across your knitting is called Fair Isle, Jacquard, or Stranded knitting.

When knitting rugs with two colors in a row, you should weave the unused color as you go. This prevents the yarns from tangling and creates a smooth, neat back for your knitting.

Working with both hands, hold the main color in your right hand (English style) and the contrast color in your left hand (Continental style), as in figure 1. This sounds complicated, but after a bit of practice it is much faster than dropping and picking up a different color every few stitches.

For a dense fabric, knit no more than two or three stitches without weaving the unused yarn. If you leave longer strands, or floats, on the back of your work, they may draw your knitting in too tightly or accidentally pull if you don't line your rug.

Again, hold the most frequently used color in your right hand. To weave the yarn not in use:

1. Lift the index finger of your left hand so the yarn held there is above the working yarn and knit one or two stitches, as in figure 2.

2. Move the yarn in your left hand below the working yarn and knit the next stitch normally.

Weaving in the ends as you go saves time at the end of the project. You can just snip the yarns close to the back of the work. Hold the new color with the unused color and weave both together as you knit.

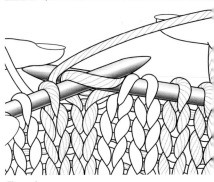

Figure 1

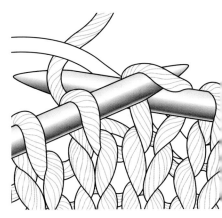

Figure 2

INTARSIA COLOR KNITTING

The knitting technique used to create large blocks of color is called intarsia. Each color is worked with a separate ball of yarn, and the yarns are crossed at the color change to lock the sections together.

Note: When working small motifs, wind off a small amount of yarn for each color, and let the yarns hang loose at the back of your work. If the yarns get tangled, you can easily separate them if they are not attached to balls.

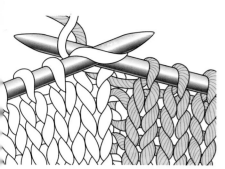
Figure 1: Right Side

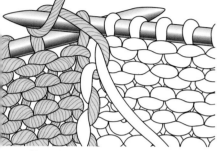
Figure 2: Wrong Side

To change colors in the middle of a row:

1. With the first color, knit up to the color change, then drop the first color.

2. Pick up the second color, crossing the yarn underneath the first color, as in figures 1 and 2. Work the first stitch tightly. Give the end of the old color a slight tug to lock the colors together, then continue knitting with the second color.

C. MOSAIC (SLIP-STITCH) COLOR KNITTING

Mosaic color knitting is an illusion. You only knit with one color on each row, but the final result looks very similar to Fair Isle knitting.

On mosaic charts:

☞ Each row on the chart stands for two rows of knitting.

☞ Each wrong side row is identical to the previous right side row.

☞ The working color is used for two full rows.

☞ The squares on the right and left edges of the chart represent the color that is used as the working yarn in those two rows.

To knit a mosaic pattern:

1. On RS rows, knit the stitches in the working color. Slip the stitches of the non-working color to the right needle with the yarn held in back, as in figure 1.

2. On WS rows, purl the stitches in the working color. Slip the stitches of the non-working color to the right needle with the yarn held in front, as in figure 2.

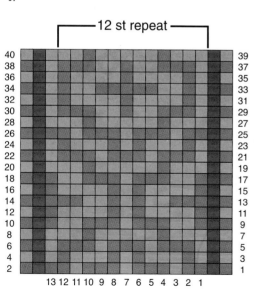

12 st repeat

40 | | | | | | | | | | | | | 39
38 | | | | | | | | | | | | | 37
36 | | | | | | | | | | | | | 35
34 | | | | | | | | | | | | | 33
32 | | | | | | | | | | | | | 31
30 | | | | | | | | | | | | | 29
28 | | | | | | | | | | | | | 27
26 | | | | | | | | | | | | | 25
24 | | | | | | | | | | | | | 23
22 | | | | | | | | | | | | | 21
20 | | | | | | | | | | | | | 19
18 | | | | | | | | | | | | | 17
16 | | | | | | | | | | | | | 15
14 | | | | | | | | | | | | | 13
12 | | | | | | | | | | | | | 11
10 | | | | | | | | | | | | | 9
8 | | | | | | | | | | | | | 7
6 | | | | | | | | | | | | | 5
4 | | | | | | | | | | | | | 3
2 | | | | | | | | | | | | | 1

13 12 11 10 9 8 7 6 5 4 3 2 1

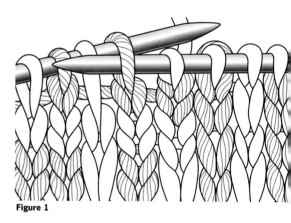
Figure 1

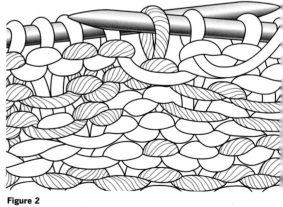
Figure 2

Note: Run the unused yarn up the side of your knitting. Drop the old color and pick up the new color from behind it. This will save you from having to join the yarn after every two rows.

TECHNIQUES USED IN TEXTURE RUGS

This section includes techniques used on projects in the section on Texture Rugs, beginning on page 113.

FELTING

Felt is a thick, matted fabric created by abusing yarns from certain natural animal fibers such as 100 percent wool or a blend of wool and mohair. Machine washable wool ("superwash"), cotton, silk, and man-made fibers will not felt, but can be used along with a strand of wool to create interesting textures.

When you knit for felting, your gauge should be very loose so you can see space between the stitches. You can't have knitting too loose for felting, but if your stitches are too tight, the piece may not felt as much as you'd like.

What rugs can you felt? I've designed two rugs specifically to be felted—the Pastel Felted Rug (page 115) and the Felted Basketweave Design (page 119), but you can felt any rug as long as you follow these guidelines:

☞ Yarn—choose a yarn that is lighter in weight than the pattern calls for (because it will thicken up when you felt it), and make sure it is "feltable."

☞ Gauge—work the design at a very loose gauge so the stitches are light and airy.

☞ Swatch first—it's always better to experiment with felting on a small piece than to spend weeks or months working on a project only to be disappointed if it doesn't felt correctly.

To felt a knitted rug, put it in a zippered pillowcase (to catch the lint), and toss it in the washing machine. Set the machine for the smallest load size with hot wash, cold rinse, and add a small amount of soap. Check the felting every five minutes. Some yarns will felt within the first few minutes, while others may take two or three cycles.

When the fibers are matted and you don't want the rug to shrink any more, take it out, and gently rinse it in tepid water in the sink. Roll the rug in a towel, and squeeze out the excess water.

CABLES

Cables add an extra level of textural interest to knitting. Cables are made when stitches in the knitted fabric cross over each other. You simply place a few stitches on hold by slipping them onto a cable needle, knit the next two or three stitches, then knit the stitches off the cable needle. These traveling stitches may move to the right or to the left.

Cable needles are short, double-pointed needles made especially for the purpose of knitting cables. They usually have a notch, ridges, or a curved section to keep the stitches from falling off while you are manipulating the cable.

This is what the Felted Basketweave Design (page 119) looked like before it was felted (WS shown).

Tip

Walking on the wrapped-up rug is quicker than squeezing with your hands.

Tip

You can let the rug continue to shrink by continuing to put it through the rinse and spin cycles in the machine.

1. Knit. It may be cliché, but "practice makes perfect"—or at least "proficient." The more you knit, the more automatic it becomes.

2. Learn the basics. Knitting is more fun once you don't have to think about what your fingers are doing.

3. Relax and have fun. This is a hobby! If you're bored with your knitting, put it aside, and work on something else. If a project isn't fun, rip it out, and start a different one.

4. Try new techniques. There's nothing quite like mastering a new technique to boost your confidence.

5. Live within your budget. Yarns come in all price ranges. By choosing interesting colors and unique embellishments, my grandmother made beautiful items using yarns she found on sale at local shops and discount stores. You can do the same.

6. Don't be afraid to change colors, stitches, or yarns. Each pattern includes a list of the yarns and pattern stitches that I used. Let your creativity adapt my basic patterns into custom designs that fit with your décor and lifestyle.

7. Ask for help if you get stuck. Some of us learn best from text, some from pictures, and others from hands-on experimentation. If you get stuck on a technique or project, visit your local yarn shop or knitting circle. You'll find plenty of knitters ready to demonstrate techniques, give advice, and help you with your projects.

To make a left-crossing cable, hold the cable needle (cn) in the front.

Crossing a six-stitch cable to the left:

1. Slip 3 stitches to cn.

2. Hold needle in front of the work.

3. Knit next 3 stitches from left needle.

4. Knit 3 stitches from cn as in figure 1.

To make a right-crossing cable, you hold the cable needle in the back.

Crossing a six-stitch cable to the right:

1. Slip 3 stitches to cn.

2. Hold needle in back of the work.

3. Knit next 3 stitches from left needle.

4. Knit 3 stitches from cn as in figure 2.

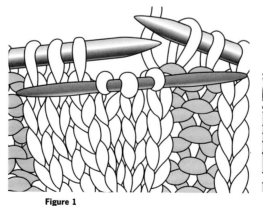

Figure 1

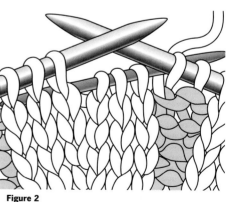

Figure 2

special techniques   42

embellishments
& accessories

Moving from a basic design to a unique work of art can be as simple as adding a personal touch. Each pattern in this book includes suggestions for finishing and embellishing, but there's no reason you can't modify the patterns to suit your own tastes. I've used a variety of techniques including knitting, crochet, and embroidery. These embellishments can be used separately or combined with beautiful results.

Tip

If you aren't satisfied with the look of a rug, don't be afraid to add embellishments. They're all easy enough to remove, so no harm's done if you don't like the results of an experiment.

EMBELLISHMENT TOOLS

Embellishments use a few tools that you may want to add to your knitting bag. Most are available at craft or fabric stores:

☞ Crochet hooks of various sizes

☞ Large-eye embroidery needles

☞ Punch or upholstery needle to add fringe or embroidery to felt

☞ Fringe cutter or piece of cardboard

☞ Rotary cutter or 9"/23cm sewing scissors

☞ Clear plastic ruler

☞ Knitted cord spool or double-pointed knitting needles of various sizes

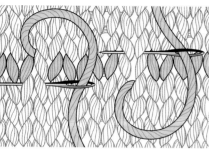

Figure 1

embellishments & accessories

EMBROIDERY

Embroidery stitches are sewn onto the surface of fabrics to add extra colors and texture. This provides an easy way to add a quick edging or to introduce small color areas that would be tedious to knit.

To embroider on knitting, thread a large-eye tapestry needle, leaving a 6"/15cm tail of yarn. Draw the embroidery yarn through the knitting from back to front, being careful to go between the knitting stitches without splitting the yarn. When finished, pull the yarn through to the back of the knitting and weave in the ends (see page 49 in Finishing Touches).

For the rugs in this book, I used two stitches—the Duplicate Stitch and the Chain Stitch—which are discussed below. An embroidery stitch book will give you many more ideas.

DUPLICATE STITCH

Duplicate stitch, or Swiss Darning, is used to add color to small areas after the knitting is complete. Because each stitch "duplicates" a knitted stitch, it looks like the design was knit in. You can work duplicate stitch horizontally, vertically, or diagonally, as in figure 1 (above).

CHAIN STITCH

Chain stitch looks like a crochet chain lying across the surface of the fabric, as in figure 2.

Chain stitch can also be worked with a crochet hook. For most people, working chain stitch with a crochet hook produces more even stitches.

1. Hold the yarn in back of the knitting.

2. From the front, insert the crochet hook through the center of a knitted stitch, and pull up a loop.

3. Insert the hook into the center of the next stitch, and pull a second loop up and through the loop on the hook, as in figure 3.

4. Repeat step 3 for desired length.

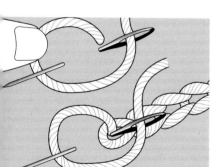

Figure 2

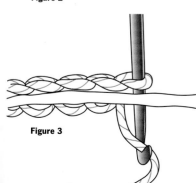

Figure 3

Note: Chain Stitch is a quick way to camouflage or decorate a seam—just work the stitches right in the join of the two pieces.

EDGES

Many knitted projects look fine with the selvage, or edge stitches at the beginning and end of each knitting row, serving as a clean border. However, there are times when the edge of a knitted piece is not neat enough for a finished edge on a rug, or when an outline of a contrasting color adds that finishing touch that makes a rug perfect. Here are some edgings I've used for the rugs in this book.

SINGLE CROCHET

Single Crochet makes a smooth edge that looks like the bind-off edge of knitting.

1. Insert a crochet hook into a stitch on the edge of the rug, and draw a loop through to the front. Wrap the yarn around the hook, and draw a second loop through the first to secure.

2. Working from right to left, insert the crochet hook into the next stitch on the edge of the rug.

3. Pull the working yarn through to the front. Two loops are now on the hook.

4. Pull the working yarn through both loops on the hook.

5. One loop remains on the hook, as in figure 4. Repeat steps 2 to 4 until the entire edge is covered.

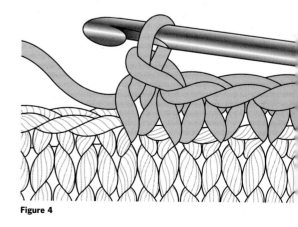

Figure 4

CRAB STITCH

Crab Stitch—also known as reverse single crochet because it is worked in the opposite direction—creates a decorative beaded edge. Crab stitch can be worked as an edging on its own, or after a row of single crochet for a wider border.

1. Insert a crochet hook into a stitch on the edge of the rug, and draw a loop through to the front. Wrap the yarn around the hook, and draw a second loop through the first to secure.

2. Working from left to right, insert the crochet hook into the next stitch on the edge of the rug.

3. Pull the working yarn through to the front. Be careful not to pull it through the loop already on the hook. Two loops are now on the hook.

4. Pull the working yarn through both loops on the hook, as in figure 5.

5. One loop remains on the hook. Repeat steps 2 to 4 until the entire edge is covered.

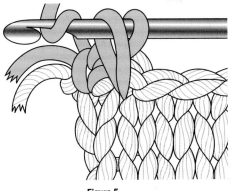

Figure 5

PICK-UP AND BIND-OFF EDGING

For those knitters who don't crochet, a pick-up and bind-off edging looks like a row of single crochet, but is made with knitting needles.

1. With the right side facing, pick up stitches along the edge of the rug.

2. Bind off, knitting all stitches.

See instructions on picking up stitches (page 36) and binding off in pattern (page 29).

Note: For a circular or oval rug, bind off with a needle two sizes larger than the needle you used for knitting the rug.

KNITTED CORD

Knitted Cord is a long, thin tube of knitting, usually made on three or four stitches. You can create a beautiful edge for a rug by sewing one or two lengths of cord onto the edge of a rug.

1. With a double-pointed needle, cast on three or four stitches.

2. Knit all stitches. Do not turn.

3. Slide the stitches to opposite end of the needle.

4. Repeat steps 2 and 3 for desired length. Bind off.

Note: You can also make knitted cord using a spool or "knitting knobby" available at most knitting or craft stores. They come with instructions and are easy to use.

Sew the knitted cord onto the edges of the rug.

1. With wrong sides facing, whipstitch the knitted cord to the outside edge of the rug. Make sure the cord does not twist.

2. Seam the two ends of the cord together.

(See page 50 in Finishing Touches for instructions on sewing seams.)

Tip

If you don't want to make your own edging for your rug, or if you want to make your rug match other décor in your house exactly, you can sew on purchased edgings, such as fringes, tassels, or cords.

FRINGES

Fringes are popular edgings for rugs. They are easy to make and can turn an ordinary rug into an attractive accessory for your home.

BASIC FRINGE

A basic fringe is made by adding strands of yarn evenly spread out across the ends of a rug or around the whole perimeter.

1. Cut two to four strands of yarn twice the length of the finished fringe and fold in half.

2. Insert a crochet hook through a stitch at the edge of the rug, and draw through a loop from the center of the folded fringe.

3. Draw the ends of the fringe strands through the folded loop, and tug gently on the ends to secure, as in figure 1.

4. Trim using a clear plastic ruler and rotary cutter.

Figure 1

BRUSHED FRINGE

To make a brushed fringe, follow instructions for a basic fringe, and separate the strands of the yarn by combing the ends of the fringe with a dog comb. This works best on multistranded yarns made from plant fibers such as cotton, jute, or hemp.

Tassels are a bit fancier than simple fringes and can be added to the corners of a rug or along the entire edge to enhance the design. Tassels and fringes can also be used together.

BASIC TASSEL

A basic tassel is made from of a cluster of yarn, fastened at one end.

1. Cut a piece of cardboard ½"/1.5cm longer than the finished tassel.

2. Wrap yarn around the cardboard 25 times or until it's as full as you like.

Note: Only half of the tassel is on one side of the cardboard, it will be twice as thick when finished.

3. Thread a piece of yarn 6"/15cm between the cardboard and the yarn loops, and tie a knot. Use these tails to sew the tassel to the rug.

4. Slip the loops off the cardboard.

5. Bind the tassel near the top, just below the hanging loop:

☞ Wrap a piece of yarn 10"/25cm long around the top of the tassel several times ½"/1.5cm from the top.

☞ Thread both tails in a needle, and hide them in the center of the tassel.

6. Cut open the bottom loops, and trim the ends evenly.

Note: If you prefer loops at the bottom of your tassel, don't cut the strands open.

TWISTED CORD TASSEL

A tassel can also be made from a twisted cord.

1. Cut two lengths of yarn about five times the length of the finished tassel, and knot both ends.

Note: Use several strands to make a thicker cord from lightweight yarn.

2. Attach one end over a hook or doorknob.

3. Twist the two strands together until they begin to kink.

4. Remove the other end of the yarn from the hook, and fold the yarn in half.

5. Holding the yarn in the center, bring both ends together allowing the strands to twist back on themselves in the opposite direction.

6. Secure the open end of the tassel with a knot, and trim evenly.

7. With a separate strand of yarn, sew the tassel to the rug at the folded end.

HOME DÉCOR ACCESSORIES

If you're like me, you'll want to coordinate your knitted rugs with other accessories in your home. There are many simple ways this can be done.

PILLOWS

Pillows are quick and easy projects—after you've made one, you'll soon believe Pillow Rule #1: You Always Need Another Pillow! If you're a new knitter and still feeling timid about making a large rug, make a pillow first. It's a good idea to make a pillow as a test before committing to a larger project, and the nicest way to use up the extra yarn that is often left over from color-work projects is to make matching pillows.

To make a pillow, knit two pieces the same size as your pillow form.

Note: Pillow forms come as squares and circles between 12 and 18"/30 x 46cm, and in rectangles about 12 x 16"/30 x 40.5cm. If you've already made your swatches, take them to a craft or fabric store to see what size pillow form is the best fit.

For rectangular or square pillows, cast on the correct number of stitches for the width of your pillow form, and work even until each piece is the height of the pillow.

If your gauge is:	2	2.5	3	3.5	4	sts/inch
For a 14"/35.5cm wide pillow, cast on:	30	38	44	52	58	sts
For a 16"/40.5cm wide pillow, cast on:	34	42	50	58	66	sts
For an 18"/46cm wide pillow, cast on:	38	48	56	66	74	sts

If your swatch is too small for the pillow form, add a few rows of crochet or knitted cord around the edge.

If your swatch is too big for the pillow form, let the edges extend past the pillow form, and sew on decorative buttons to close the pillow.

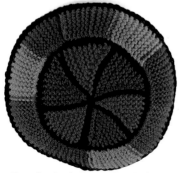

For a classically simple pillow, attach the sides together by sewing.

For a fancier design, work a single-crochet edge, or attach fringes all the way around the pillow, going through both pieces of knitting at the same time.

For a circular pillow, start from the center using one of the designs for circular rugs, and continue until your piece is the same size as the pillow form.

Attach the pieces together on three sides, then insert the pillow form before closing the fourth side.

Note: You can make the front and back the same, or make the front to match your rug, and knit an easy Garter Stitch piece for the back.

WALL HANGINGS AND PORTIERES

You can make just about any knitted rug into an ornamental wall hanging or a portiere (doorway covering) to keep cold drafts from spreading throughout your house in the winter.

KNITTING A CASING

The easiest way to hang a knitted rug is by adding a casing so you can insert a dowel or curtain rod as a hanger.

1. With the WS facing, pick up and knit stitches along the purl bumps one row below the top edge of the rug.

Note: Do not pick up the edge stitches themselves or the casing will show on the right side.

2. Work in Stockinette St until the casing is large enough to fit over a dowel or curtain rod.

3. Do not bind off. Whipstitch the open stitches to the back of the rug.

Tip

If your rug is heavy, line it first to keep the knitted fabric from stretching out of shape. For instructions on lining rugs, see page 53 in Finishing Touches.

For a decorative hanger, make a twisted cord, and attach it to both ends of the dowel with tassels.

finishing touches

After you complete knitting and embellishment, you're ready to prepare your rug for use or display. The type of finishing you should choose depends on the fiber used and the ultimate purpose for your rug.

PUTTING YOUR RUG TOGETHER

Every knitting project has tails of yarn hanging out all over the back. Some rugs are also made from multiple pieces that are sewn together, leaving even more ends of yarn. Whatever you do, don't cut these ends off. To finish your rugs, you need to secure the ends and sew the seams.

WEAVING IN THE ENDS

To keep your rug from unraveling or falling apart, you must weave in the ends to secure them.

1. Thread the tail onto a blunt tapestry needle.

2. On the wrong side, weave the tail in and out of the bumps on the back of the fabric (figure 1):

☞ Weave in one direction for a few inches, then turn and work in the opposite direction for about 1"/2.5cm.

☞ When working with a double strand of yarn, weave in the two tails separately so they don't make a bulge in your rug.

3. Trim the tail to ½"/1.5cm.

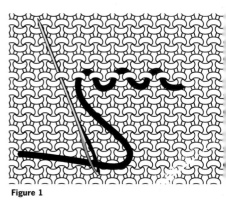

Figure 1

Note: If your yarn frays easily, seal the ends with a liquid seam sealant, available at most craft or fabric stores. Alternatively, tie a knot near the end of the tail.

SEWING SEAMS

Rugs made from strips or patches must be sewn together. I used three different types of seams for my rugs: invisible seams, whipstitch seams, and end-to-end seams.

INVISIBLE SEAMS

Invisible seams, also known as mattress stitch seams, are sewn on the right side. The invisible seam joins two pieces of knitting together, and the finished rug appears as if it were knit as one large piece. Invisible seams are sewn differently on Garter Stitch and Stockinette Stitch.

To sew an invisible seam on Garter Stitch (see figure 2):

1. With the right sides of the fabric facing up, place the two pieces to be seamed on a flat surface.

2. With a tapestry needle and matching yarn, catch the bump on the edge of one piece of knitting.

3. Repeat step 2 on the other piece.

Note: To make the seam completely invisible, catch the top bump of each ridge on one piece of knitting and the bottom bump on the other.

4. Continue to work from side to side, pulling gently on the yarn to close the seam every 2"/5cm.

To sew an invisible seam on Stockinette Stitch (see figure 3):

1. With the right sides facing up, place the two pieces to be seamed on a flat surface.

2. With a tapestry needle and matching yarn, go under the bar between first and second stitches near the edge of one piece of knitting.

Note: Make your stitches one-half stitch (for very bulky yarn) or one stitch (for lighter yarn) in from the edge.

3. Repeat step 2 on the other piece.

Note: For a quicker seam, catch two bars from each side as you make each stitch.

4. Continue to work from side to side, pulling gently on the yarn to close the seam every 2"/5cm.

WHIPSTITCH SEAMS

Whipstitch seams can be sewn on either the right side or the wrong side.

☞ When sewn on the wrong side, the two edges of the knitted pieces remain distinct on the right side, leaving a clear ridge between the strips or patches.

☞ When sewn on the right side, whipstitch makes a flat seam that is neat and decorative.

Whipstitch is sewn in the same way on any fabric, and can also be used to join pieces knit in different directions. (See figure 4.)

1. With the right or wrong sides of the fabric facing up (your choice), place the two pieces to be seamed on a flat surface.

2. With a tapestry needle and matching or contrasting yarn, use one smooth motion to catch the stitch on the edge of one piece of knitting and then catch a stitch on the other piece.

3. Continue along the seam, pulling gently on the yarn to close the seam every 2"/5cm.

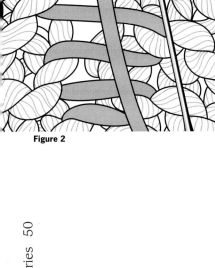
Figure 2

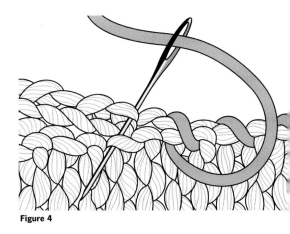
Figure 4

Figure 3

Whipstitch can also be used to sew fabric linings to knitting. Just "take a bite" of the fabric in place of catching a knitted stitch. See page 53 in this chapter for instructions on lining rugs.

Note: On pieces with curved seams that may not be exactly the same size, ease the pieces-that is catch two bumps on the longer piece every few stitches to make the pieces line up smoothly.

END-TO-END SEAMS

End-to-end seams are used to join the cast-on and bound-off edges of knit pieces.

1. With the right sides of the fabric facing up, place the two pieces to be seamed on a flat surface.

2. With a tapestry needle and matching yarn, catch the knit V just inside the edge of one piece of knitting.

Note: In garter stitch, catch the V just below the garter ridge, and the seam will disappear between the ridges.

3. Repeat step 2 on the other piece.

4. Continue to work from side to side, pulling gently on the yarn to close the seam after each stitch (See figure 5).

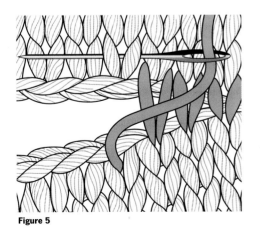

Figure 5

Note: The seam should be at the same tension as your knitting, and look like a row of stockinette stitch.

BLOCKING RUGS

Blocking, either by washing or steaming knitted pieces, evens out the stitches, and creates a flat, smooth texture. While blocking is not always needed for a rug to lie flat, it will make your finished piece look neater and more professional.

The type of fiber and stitch patterns used on the rug will determine the best method of blocking. The bands on the balls of most knitting yarns include blocking recommendations. Check these instructions before treating any yarn. Wash and block your swatch in the way you intend to treat the finished rug to make sure you like the results.

WET BLOCKING

Washing a rug to relax the knitted fabric works especially well on cables and other knit-and-purl stitch patterns where pressing the rug would flatten out the texture. This wash-and-block technique is safe for any type of yarn, and is an easy way to relax a large knitted piece without much muscle work.

1. Soak the rug in cool water in the washing machine for 15 minutes, or until the fiber is saturated. If desired, use a no-rinse wool-washing solution.

2. Spin out the excess water, making sure the washer is also set for a cool rinse.

3. Remove the rug from the washer, and lay it out flat to dry.

If the rug is still not lying perfectly flat, you may decide to pin it in place as it dries (use rust-proof pins), or steam press while it is still damp.

STEAM BLOCKING

Steaming works well to even out the stitches on color work and plain Stockinette stitch, which may seem uneven or even sloppy before blocking, and to soften and relax yarns that are particularly stiff or energized.

Note: You can also steam pieces that don't lie perfectly flat because of unusual shaping.

1. Wet and wring out an old towel.

2. Lay the rug flat on a padded surface.

3. Lightly press the piece through the towel, letting the steam penetrate the fibers.

Note: Occasionally, you may want to press a piece more firmly. Always test this on a swatch before trying it on your finished rug!

BLOCKING A FELTED RUG

To block a felted rug, lay it out on a flat surface, tug at it to straighten out the sides and reshape the edging. Press it with lots of steam through a towel, then leave it to dry. This may take a few days, so be patient.

BACKING RUGS

Backing rugs with nonstick material gives them an extra layer of protection and, in the case of pile rugs, can keep the pile from coming loose. You can also apply fabric as a backing, or place a rug on a commercial rug pad.

APPLYING NONSLIP BACKINGS TO PILE RUGS

Most rug-hooking and craft suppliers carry liquid latex products made for backing hooked rugs. This makes a perfect backing for knitted pile rugs.

1. Place the rug face down on a clean work surface protected by a drop cloth.

2. Stretching the rug so it lies flat but is not distorted, pin it onto the surface with rust-proof pins.

3. Follow the directions on the package, covering only the section of pile knitting (not the rug edging).

4. Allow the latex to dry thoroughly before unpinning or moving the rug.

APPLYING NONSLIP BACKINGS TO RUGS WITHOUT PILE

The puffy fabric paint sold in most craft stores makes a great nonslip backing for rugs without pile. The paint can be applied directly to the knitted fabric, or onto a sewn-on lining. Follow the manufacturer's instructions.

Note: Try blow-drying instead of ironing to "puff" the paint.

USING COMMERCIAL RUG BACKINGS

If you don't want to attach a nonslip surface or lining to your rug, you can place a commercial rug pad, or "underlayment," under your rug. Some of these pads, available in natural or manmade materials, are custom cut by the manufacturer; others can be cut to the desired size and shape with scissors.

Tip

Don't steam or press manmade fibers or novelty yarns. Steam blocking has no permanent effect on acrylic because the yarn returns to its original shape when it is washed and dried. In addition, if too much heat is applied to man-made fibers, they may melt.

Painting latex on the back of a rug will hold pile or loops in place and make a skid-proof surface.

You can find rug pads in home décor specialty shops and home improvement stores.

Floor rugs, particularly unlined reversible rugs, should be placed on a rug pad for durability and to prevent slipping.

LINING RUGS

Linings add protection to the back of knitted rugs and will keep the flexible knitted fabric from stretching out of shape.

1. Purchase backing fabric and sewing thread that matches your rug. Wash and dry the fabric to preshrink it.

2. Cut the fabric to the finished shape and size of the rug, not counting fringes or tassels, plus a 1½"/4cm hem allowance.

3. Fold the hem allowance under and press:

☞ For square, rectangular, or hexagon-shaped rugs, fold the hem allowance under on all sides and press, as in figure 1.

☞ For oval or circular rugs, clip the hem evenly around the circumference of the lining to ease in the extra fabric and press, as in figure 2.

4. Place the rug facedown on a clean, flat working surface, and pin the lining right side up on top of it, with all edges even, and pin in place.

5. Whipstitch by hand around the edges of the rug using matching sewing thread (figure 3). (Machine stitching creates a channel that weakens knitting, and may also stretch the rug out of shape.)

Note: Make sure your stitches go through the lining and the knitting, but don't show on the right side.

6. Tack the lining to the body of the rug at even intervals to keep the lining from shifting. (See figure 3.)

7. Remove the pins, and press the lining lightly.

To quilt a rug, place batting between the knitting and lining fabric. Cut the batting to the finished size of the rug with no additional hem allowance. Rugs can also be backed with sewn-on fabric linings made from regular fabric or nonslip material.

For a decorative accent, use yarn to tack the lining to the rug. Sew the yarn through all layers with a sharp needle, then secure the ends by tying a square knot on the back of the rug. Trim the yarn to about ½"/1.5cm.

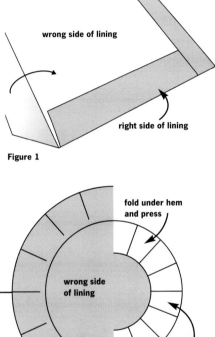

wrong side of lining

right side of lining

Figure 1

fold under hem and press

slits

wrong side of lining

right side of lining

hem

Figure 2

fornt of rug (gray)

back of rug

Figure 3

CARING FOR HAND-KNIT RUGS

Treat your hand-knit rug as you would any other work of art, with regular care and maintenance.

☞ Remove loose dirt from your rug by shaking it out gently.

☞ Blot up spills immediately.

☞ Vacuum with a hand attachment, but don't use a beater bar.

PRETREATING HAND-KNIT RUGS

You may want to protect your rug from stains, UV fading, fire, and moths by pretreating them with spray-on or wash-in fabric treatments, available at most craft or fabric stores. Your dry cleaner may also be able to apply many of these treatments for you.

WASHING RUGS

Contrary to popular belief, wool, cotton, and other natural fibers can be safely washed in the machine.

1. Fill the washing machine with cool water and a small amount of pH-neutral no-rinse wool wash (available at most yarn shops).

Note: After the washer is full, turn it off so it does not enter the agitation cycle. If rugs made of wool are allowed to agitate, they will felt and shrink.

2. After shaking any loose dirt out of the rug, gently submerge the rug under the water, and let it soak for 15 to 20 minutes.

3. Switch the washer to the spin cycle to remove the excess water.

4. Remove the rug from the washer, and lay it out flat to dry. Be careful to support the weight of the rug as you move it, so it doesn't stretch out of shape.

5. If desired, press the rug lightly through a towel. (See page 52 in this chapter for instructions on pressing hand-knit rugs.)

STORING RUGS

Rugs are best stored flat, but that is not always possible, particularly with larger pieces. Always clean rugs thoroughly before putting them into storage.

Store rugs in a well-ventilated, cool location out of direct sunlight.

☞ Store rugs flat or roll them. Don't fold them, or you might end up with permanent creases or discoloration at the fold lines.

☞ Don't store rugs in the basement or attic because temperature and humidity fluctuations can damage the fibers and promote mildew.

☞ Don't store rugs directly on the floor as this may attract carpet beetles. Cedar chests or other airtight containers will keep moth larvae out.

☞ Even textile experts such as museum curators and antique dealers don't all agree whether cedar chips, dried lavender, or eucalyptus leaves actually repel clothing moths, but they do make your rugs smell great. Don't use chemical mothballs, even if they are scented to mask the horrid smell. Up to 95 percent of typical moth-ball products consist of toxic chemicals that can damage the rug and are dangerous to children or pets.

☞ If you do see moths, put the rug in the freezer for three or four days to kill the larvae. Then shake out and wash the rug.

3. Check your rug frequently to be sure it is free from pests, moisture, and other damage.

tips for rolling rugs

☞ Roll pile rugs with latex backing with the pile to the outside.

☞ Roll flat-knit rugs wrong side out.

☞ Roll the rug in acid-free tissue paper.

☞ Don't roll the rug in plastic because it holds in moisture and promotes mildew.

☞ Wrap the rug in muslin, or pack it in an acid-free textile storage tube, or in a regular cardboard tube lined with acid-free paper.

RUGS AS GIFTS

Once you've made your first rug an amazing thing happens—your friends start dropping not-so-subtle hints about how much they'd love to have a knitted rug, too. This is a cue, of course, for you to share this book with them and teach them how to make a rug for themselves. If that's not feasible, or if you want to give a surprise gift, then follow these few tips to make sure your gift is appreciated and cared for.

☛ Match your gift rug to the recipient's décor.

☛ If you're unsure about the suitability of a rug as a gift, make a pillow first.

☛ Personalize your gift by "signing" it with a stitch-on label with your name as the artist.

☛ Include care and storage instructions.

☛ Keep a journal of birthdays and other special events so you properly schedule enough time to make your intended gifts. You want to enjoy creating your gift as much as your recipients enjoy using it.

ABOUT THE PROJECTS

On the next pages you'll find 21 projects, presented in five categories of knitted rug techniques: Easy Garter Stitch, Knit-and-Purl, Pile, Color-Work, and Texture. There are rugs to appeal to the very new knitter, as well as to those who are quite experienced. It is my hope that, whatever your skill level, you will take my designs as a springboard for your own creations, playing with different color combinations and exciting new yarns, and experimenting with different techniques.

Happy knitting!

easy garter stitch rugs

Garter Stitch is the simplest stitch in knitting: you knit every stitch in every row. With no purls or tricky finger acrobatics, this is the most basic knitted fabric you can create. Each two rows knit in Garter Stitch makes a well-defined ridge in the fabric. These ridges are easy to see and count, so keeping track of your knitting is effortless.

Even though—or because—it's so simple, Garter Stitch is very versatile and you can use it to create many different patterns and shapes.

The resulting fabric has some very special properties that make it stand out. The height of two rows of knitting—one garter ridge—equals the width of one stitch. Also, the fabric is very flexible, and when knit in strips can be molded into different shapes. Garter stitch is thicker than most other stitches, making it perfect for projects that will end up under-foot. What's more, the knitting is reversible, so keeping track of the right side is not always important.

If all you know how to do is cast on and do the knit stitch, you can make all of the rugs in this section. Any new techniques are included with the patterns. If you're a more experienced knitter, you'll have fun experimenting with the endless variety and options that you can craft with beautiful yarns and a pinch of imagination.

Quick-Knit Garter Stitch Trio

A simple Garter Stitch rug is a perfect project for beginners—or anyone needing a quick gift—because you can knit one in a weekend. This vibrant rug is made using just the knit stitch and a double strand of heavy yarn on jumbo needles. The design variations show how using different yarns and colors creates completely different-looking rugs.

Finished Measurements
Approx 24 x 36"/61 x 91cm blocked, without fringe

Materials
Yarn: super bulky yarn

　　Color A (hand-painted), 465yd/425m
　　Color B (gold), 155yd/142m

Knitting needles: 12mm (size 17 U.S.) circular needle, at least 73.5cm/29" long *or size to obtain gauge*

Blunt tapestry needle for weaving in ends and sewing seams if made in strips

Gauge
Approx 6 sts and 12 rows = 4"/10cm over Garter st using a double strand of yarn

Your exact gauge will vary depending on the yarn you choose.

Pattern Note
Knitting large projects can be easier and less cumbersome if you make narrow strips instead of one wide piece of knitting. This rug and the solid blue one are knit in one piece. The periwinkle and mulberry rug is made of three separate pieces sewn together after the knitting is complete.

Pattern Stitch
Garter Stitch

Knit every stitch in every row.

Instructions

1. With a double strand of yarn, cast on 36 sts.

Note: Be very careful to catch both strands of yarn in every stitch.

2. Work in Garter st for 36"/91cm, following stripe pattern:

12 rows color A (hand-painted)
12 rows color B (gold)
12 rows color A (hand-painted)
16 rows color B (gold)

Knit in color A (hand-painted) until piece measures 27"/69cm from beginning.

16 rows color B (gold)
12 rows color A (hand-painted)
12 rows color B (gold)
12 rows color A (hand-painted)

Note: When working Garter st in stripes, always start a new color on a right side (RS) row.

3. Bind off.

Rag Rug Tip

This simple stitch pattern and shape are perfect for experimenting with rag rugs. Almost any type of fabric will work well, but your rug will be a different size if you don't achieve my gauge.

Finishing

Weave in the ends and block to measurements. Add fringe or twisted cord tassels if desired. See Embellishment & Accessories on page 46 for instructions on making fringes and tassels.

This rug was knit with
Cherry Tree *Hill Yarn's Plush*, 100% Cotton Chenille, 155yd/142m per hank.
(A) 1 hank, Peacock
(B) 3 hanks, Loden

Variation

Three Strips

I made this rug in three strips with different stripe patterns. You can make as many strips as you like. They can be all the same width or different. To make a wider strip, cast on more stitches. To make a narrow strip, cast on fewer stitches.

Materials

Yarn: super bulky yarn

Color A (periwinkle): 399yd/365m
Color B (mulberry): 228yd/208m

Instructions

Strips (make three)

1. With a double strand of yarn, cast on 12 sts.

2. Work in Garter st for 36"/91cm, working random stripe patterns, using different combinations for added interest:

2 strands of Color A (periwinkle)
2 strands of Color B (mulberry)
1 strand of Color A and 1 strand of Color B held together

3. Bind off.

4. Arrange the strips in an interesting pattern and whipstitch the seams together on the wrong side. This makes a nice ridge where the strips join so the colors don't blur together.

Note: If you prefer a more blended effect, work invisible seams.

For seam instructions, see page 50 in Finishing Touches.

This rug was knit with
Classic Elite's *Waterspun Weekend*, 100% Merino Wool, 57yd/52m per ball:
(A) 7 skeins, Periwinkle #7292
(B) 4 skeins, Mulberry #7299

Variation

Solid Blue

This rug can be made with any type of super bulky yarn you like. For a plush rug, use a soft, lofty wool or a novelty yarn. For a harder-wearing rug, heavy cotton yarn or sturdy rug wool make good yarn choices. The simplicity of the design shows off the texture of the different yarns, making it easy to "design your own."

Materials

Yarn: super bulky yarn approx 610yd/558m

Instructions

1. With a double strand of yarn, cast on 36 sts.

Note: Be very careful to catch both strands of yarn in every stitch.

2. Work in Garter st for 36"/91cm.

3. Bind off.

This rug was knit with
12 skeins of Classic Elite's *Weekend Cotton*, 100% Mercerized Cotton, 51yd/47m per ball, Blue #4892

Simple Shaker Pinwheel

This rug was inspired by the elaborate circular rugs knit by Shaker Sisters in the early 1900s. A simpler version than the famous vintage rugs, it combines the traditional pinwheel center and concentric circle pattern with bright contemporary colors.

Finished Measurements
Approx 42"/107cm diameter after sewing and blocking, including crochet border

Materials
Yarn: super bulky yarn

Color A (black), 186 yd/170m
Color B (purple), 248 yd/226m
Color C (red), 248 yd/226m
Color D (light green), 124 yd/113m
Color E (dark green), 124 yd/113m

Knitting needles: 6mm (size 10 U.S.) *or size to obtain gauge*

6mm (Size J/10 U.S.) crochet hook for edging

Tapestry needle for weaving in ends and sewing seams

Gauge
8 st strip = approx 2.5"/7cm wide, over Garter st

Always take time to check your gauge.

Pattern Notes
On the pinwheel center:

RS (odd) rows are worked out from the center toward the edge.

WS (even) rows are worked in from the edge of the circle toward the center.

Work every other wedge with a different color.

Slip stitches as if to knit with yarn in back (wyib). See page 35 for instructions on slipping stitches.

Pattern Stitch
Garter Stitch

Knit every stitch in every row.

Instructions

Pinwheel Center
Note: The pinwheel center looks like six separate wedges, but you actually knit it as one circular piece, changing colors after each wedge.

1. First wedge. With color A (black), cast on 10 sts. Knit one row (setup row, WS). Change to color B (purple).

Row 1 and odd rows through row 15 (RS): Sl 1 st as if to knit. Knit to end of row.
Row 2 (WS): K9 turn.
Row 4: K8 turn.
Row 6: K7 turn.
Row 8: K6 turn.
Row 10: K5 turn.
Row 12: K4 turn.
Row 14: K3 turn.
Row 16: K2 turn.
Row 17: Sl 1, k1.
Row 18: K across all 10 stitches.
Rows 19 and 20: With color A (black), k 2 rows.

2. Wedges 2-5. Repeat rows 1-20 four times, alternating colors B (purple) and C (red) for each repeat.

3. Wedge 6. Using color C (red), repeat rows 1-18 one final time.

4. Bind off knit-wise. Sew cast-on to bind-off edge. See page 50 in Finishing Touches for instructions on sewing end to end seams.

5. Using color A (black), work 1 row of single crochet around outside edge of circle. Set center pinwheel aside. See page 44 in Embellishment & Accessories for instructions on crocheting edgings.

Strips

For each of the four strips, cast on 8 sts and work in Garter st, changing colors as indicated below. Each strip is longer than the previous strip. Repeat the stripe pattern the number of times indicated. When you complete the stripe pattern, bind off and sew the ends of the strip together to make a big "O".

Note: Remember that each ridge in Garter st is two rows, and you'll have an easier time counting.

1. Knit first strip with this stripe pattern:

20 rows color D (light green)
20 rows color E (dark green)
22 rows color B (purple)

Repeat stripe pattern three times. Bind off and sew ends together with color D (light green).

Note: I used the wrong side of this strip for the front because I thought the color changes were more interesting.

2. Knit second strip with this stripe pattern:

54 rows color C (red)
54 rows color B (purple)

Repeat stripe pattern three times. Bind off and sew ends together using color C (red).

3. Knit third strip with this stripe pattern:

8 rows color B (purple)
16 rows color C (red)
8 rows color B (purple)
16 rows color D (light green)
8 rows color B (purple)
16 rows color C (red)
8 rows color B (purple)
16 rows color E (dark green)

Repeat stripe pattern four times. Bind off and sew ends together using color B (purple).

4. Knit fourth strip. This strip is too long to count rows! Knit with color D (light green) until your strip reaches halfway around the rug. Then change to color E (dark green), and knit the second half. Bind off and sew ends together using color D (light green).

Finishing

Sewing

See page 50 in Finishing Techniques for instructions on sewing seams.

Sew each strip onto the rug as it is completed so you can admire your work and make sure the strips fit nicely. If the strip is a tad too short, knit a few extra rows. If it's a little long, rip out a few rows. This design is so forgiving, you'll never be able to tell you cheated.

Tip
If your rug peaks in the center or ruffles around the edges, don't panic. Soak it in cool water in your washing machine, spin the excess water out, press the rug on the wrong side through a towel—and it will flatten out.

HISTORICAL TECHNIQUE

My design has the same pinwheel center as many Shaker rugs, but if you'd like to experiment with combining historical techniques, you can use a different center on yours. One easy center is made from a plain straight strip of Garter Stitch. According to instructions in some early 20th-century rugmaking books, a straight strip can be knit to exactly the right length, so when you gather one edge, it forms a flat wheel and doesn't ruffle or cup. I tested this—if you make an 8 st strip 14"/36cm long, you can gather it into a center for this rug in place of the pinwheel. This technique was often used in Amish rugs.

Try knitting this rug with strips of lightweight quilting cotton or T-shirt knits. If you use a woven fabric, double fold your strips to hide the raw edges inside. Be particularly careful to make each piece the right size as you knit, because fabric strips will not block into shape as easily as wool yarn.

Place the finished strip around the outside edge of the rug with WS facing up. Pin the strip to the rug so the garter ridges are evenly distributed around the circumference and you like the arrangement of the stripes.

Using color A (black), whipstitch the garter ridges on the strip to the single-crochet border on the previous piece. Work one row of single crochet around the new piece.

Outside Crochet Border

See page 44 in Embellishments & Accessories for instructions on crocheting edgings.

With RS facing, work nine rows of single crochet around the outside of the rug in the following stripe pattern. Increase (work two single crochets in the same stitch) as indicated.

Color A (black), 1 row
Color B (purple), 2 rows
Color C (red), 3 rows—increase 16 sts evenly spaced in each row
Color B (purple), 2 rows—increase 16 sts evenly spaced in each row
Color A (black), 1 row
With color A (black), work 1 row of Crab Stitch.

Note: Every knitter has a different gauge for crochet. Check as you go to make sure your crochet edge is not ruffling or cupping. If it is ruffling, increase fewer stitches. If it is cupping, increase more stitches.

Blocking

Weave in the ends and block. If you measured carefully and sewed your rug together as you finished each piece, it should require only light blocking.

This rug was knit with
Reynolds' *Paternayan Rug Wool*, 100% Persian wool, 62yd/57m per skein
(A) 3 skeins, Black #050
(B) 4 skeins, Purple #612
(C) 4 skeins, Red #855
(D) 2 skeins, Light green #559
(E) 2 skeins, Dark green #520

Log Cabin Quilted Rug

If you love quilts but don't have time to sew one, this classic Log Cabin
quilted rug will satisfy your desire. The yarn is a lighter-weight blend than
most of the projects in this book, but its acrylic content adds strength.
The quilt batting provides extra cushioning, prolonging the life of the rug
and making it an excellent exercise mat, too.

Finished Measurements
Approx 32 x 63"/81 x 160cm after sewing, blocking, and quilting

Materials
Yarn: medium weight yarn

    Color A (variegated), 810yd/741m
    Color B (burgundy), 1200yd/1097m
    Color C (green), 591yd/540m

Knitting needles: 4.5mm (Size 7 U.S.) *or size to obtain gauge*

2 yd/2m of cotton or polyester quilt batting, 45"/114cm wide for quilting

2 yd/2m of cotton or cotton-poly blend fabric, 45"/114cm wide, and matching sewing thread for lining

Tapestry needle for weaving in ends

Sewing needle for attaching lining

Gauge
For this rug, make the first square as your gauge swatch. Measure after you have the center section finished to see if you're on track. If not, go up or down a needle size as necessary. If you're close, there's no need to rip out and start over.

Center square = 2"/5cm, as knit

Finished square = 8"/20cm, blocked

Always take time to check your gauge.

Pattern Stitch
Garter Stitch

Knit every stitch in every row.

Pattern Note
See page 36 for instructions on picking up stitches.

Always pick up stitches with RS facing.

Instructions

Log Cabin Square (make 32)

1. With color A (variegated), cast on 10 sts. Work 20 rows of Garter st. Bind off 9 sts (1 st will still be on the needle).

2. Change to color B (burgundy).

Pick up 9 sts along left side (10 sts on the needle). Knit 9 rows ending with a WS row. Bind off 9 sts (1 st on the needle).

Pick up 14 sts along left side (15 sts on needle). Knit 9 rows ending with a WS row. Bind off 14 sts.

3. Change to color C (green).

Pick up 14 sts along left side (15 sts on the needle). Knit 9 rows ending with a WS row. Bind off 14 sts.

Pick up 19 sts along left side (20 sts on the needle). Knit 9 rows, ending with a WS row. Bind off 19 sts.

4. Change to color A (variegated)

Pick up 19 sts along left side (20 sts on the needle). Knit 9 rows ending with a RS row. Bind off 19 sts.

Pick up 24 sts along left side (25 sts on the needle). Knit 9 rows ending with a WS row. Bind off 24 sts.

5. Change to color B (burgundy)

Pick up 24 sts along left side (25 sts on the needle). Knit 9 rows ending with a WS row. Bind off 24 sts.

Pick up 29 sts along left side (30 sts on the needle). Knit 9 rows ending with a WS row. Bind off all sts.

Note: If you don't like following line-by-line instructions, follow these simple rules:

Knit the center until you have 10 Garter ridges on the RS. Knit the remaining sections until you have 5 Garter ridges on the RS.

At the end of each section, bind off all stitches but 1.

On sections where you change colors, pick up the same number of stitches.

On sections where you continue with the same color, pick up 5 more stitches.

Continue in this manner until you have 30 sts.

Finishing

Don't bother weaving in all those ends. They'll be hidden inside the quilted backing. Tie the ends together on the back, and clip them, leaving tails about $1/2$"/1.25cm long.

Using the photo to guide you, assemble the squares. Use the whipstitch on the right side for a subtle decorative seam. Line the rug, sandwiching a piece of quilt batting in between the knit top and the fabric backing. See Finishing Touches for instructions on sewing seams (page 50) and attaching linings (page 53).

This rug was knit with
Lion Brand's *Wool-Ease*, 80% acrylic/20% wool:
(A) 5 balls, 2.5oz/70g, 162yd/148m per ball, Autumn #233
(B) 3 balls, 3oz/85g, 197yd/180m per ball, Green Heather #130

Plymouth's *Encore Worsted*, 75% acrylic/25% wool:
(C) 6 balls, 3.5oz /100g, 200yd/183m per ball, color #999

Design Tip

This rug was made in four rows of eight squares each. For a smaller rug, make fewer squares. For a larger rug, such as a bed rug, make more squares–just remember to buy extra yarn if you add more squares.

Handspun Spiral

On a recent trip to New Mexico, I was mesmerized by handspun plant-dyed yarns I found there. A skein of yellow, brick, and gold called "Yellow Brick Road" inspired this spiral design. The entire rug is made in one long strip that you then coil and sew together as if you were making a basket.

Finished Measurements
Approx 28"/71cm diameter, after sewing and blocking, including knitted cord border

Materials
Yarn: medium weight yarn in wool or wool/mohair blend

Color A (variegated yellow), 162yd/148m
Color B (variegated pink), 162yd/148m
Color C (hot pink), 200yd/183m
Color D (yellow), 200yd/183m
Color E (burgundy), 400yd/366m

Knitting needles: 5.75mm (size 10 U.S.) double-pointed needles *or size to obtain gauge*

Note: You can use straight or double-pointed needles for the body of the rug, but you'll need two double-pointed needles for the knitted cord edging.

Blunt tapestry needle for sewing seams and weaving in ends

Gauge
7 st strip = approx 2¼"/6cm wide, over Garter st using a double strand of yarn

Always take time to check your gauge.

Note: Because handspun yarn may vary in thickness, the width of the strip may fluctuate, slightly changing the final size of the rug. In my rug, the strip is 2"/5cm wide in some places and 2½"/6.5cm in others.

Pattern Note
Set aside 1oz/28g of color A (yellow) for the ending wedge and 2oz/57g of Color E (burgundy) for the knitted cord edging.

Save about 10yd/9m of each color for sewing the seams. That way, you can use matching colors to seam each section.

Pattern Stitch
Garter Stitch

Knit every stitch in every row.

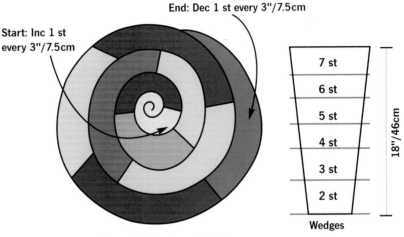

Start: Inc 1 st every 3"/7.5cm

End: Dec 1 st every 3"/7.5cm

7 st
6 st
5 st
4 st
3 st
2 st
Wedges

18"/46cm

Figure 1. Handspun Spiral

Instructions

Center Wedge
1. With a double strand of color A (yellow) cast on 2 sts.

2. Work in Garter st for 3"/7.5cm. End on a WS row.

3. On next row (RS): K1, m1, k to end of row. (For instructions on the m1 increase, see page 34.)

4. Repeat steps 2 and 3 until you have 7 sts in a row.

5. Knit even for 3"/7.5cm. Piece should measure 18"/46 cm.

Don't try to copy my rug exactly. You'll probably have a slightly different amount of each color yarn than I did. If you start with shorter segments near the center, and work longer segments near the outside, you'll end up with a rug that has a similar look to the one in the photo. Remember to make your color E (burgundy) sections about twice as long as the segments of the other colors. Don't worry if you run out of a yarn near the end, just continue with the remaining colors.

HISTORICAL TECHNIQUE

Just for fun, try arranging the colors in this rug in the hit-or-miss style that was popular in Early American and Amish rugs. Roll your yarn into balls, and put it all into a shopping bag. Whenever you feel like a change—every few rows or every few inches/cm—just reach in and grab a new color. Don't even worry about changing colors on right side rows, let the yarn design the rug for you.

Rag Rug Tip

This traditional design works well with fabric strips. Because fabric strips are not as malleable as wool yarn, you'll need to lengthen the center and ending wedges by working even for at least 12"/30cm between increases and decreases or the rug won't be flat.

Spiral Body of Rug

1. Knit even, changing yarns on RS rows as desired. This is the color sequence that I used:

10"/25cm color A (variegated yellow)
10"/25cm color B (variegated pink)
15"/38cm color C (hot pink)
30"/76cm color E (burgundy)
18"/46cm color D (yellow)
18"/46cm color A (variegated yellow)
18"/46cm color B (variegated pink)
18"/46cm color C (hot pink)
36"/91cm color E (burgundy)
18"/46cm color D (yellow)
18"/46cm color A (variegated yellow)
18"/46cm color B (variegated pink)

Ending Wedge

1. Change to reserved color A (yellow).

2. Work in Garter st for 3"/7.5 cm. End on a WS row.

3. On next row (RS), k1, k2tog, k to end of row. (For instructions on the k2tog decrease, see page 35 in Special Techniques.)

4. Repeat steps 2 and 3 until you have 2 sts.

5. Knit even for 3"/7.5cm. Ending wedge should measure 18"/46cm.

6. Bind off.

Finishing

Sew together in a spiral, using whipstitch on the WS to allow the ridges between the spiral to be more prominent. If you prefer a smoother seam, use an invisible seam on the RS. For instructions on sewing seams, see page 50 in Finishing Touches.

Note: To see what your rug looks like as you progress, sew each section as you go, instead of waiting until you finish all of the knitting.

Weave in the ends and block. To make this rug flat, you'll have to steam it heavily, or wash it and let it dry flat.

Knitted Cord Edging

With reserved color (E), work a three-stitch knitted cord for 51"/130cm, or length to reach around the outside edge of rug. For instructions on making knitted cord, see page 45 in Embellishments & Accessories.

Seam ends of knitted cord to form a ring. Then sew the knitted cord edging around the outside edge of rug.

This rug was knit with
La Lana Wools' *Forever Random*™ Blends, Obverse Blends 60% wool/40% mohair, 2oz/57g (approx 81yd/74m) per skein:
(A) 2 skeins, Yellow Brick Road
(B) 2 skeins, Sonrisa

La Lana Wools' *Millspun Knitting Worsted*, 100% Wool, 4oz/113g (approx 200yd/183m) per skein:
(C) 1 skein, Hot Stuff
(D) 1 skein, Chamisa
(E) 2 skeins, Bayeta

Note: Because many of La Lana Wools yarns are hand spun, they are measured by weight, not length. Each skein is either 2 or 4oz/57 or 114g. The yardages above are approximate because the thickness of the yarn fluctuates.

Mitered Square Patchwork

This classic patchwork design was inspired by the clean colors of Amish quilts. Like a quilt, the rug is big, but each square is small, so you can carry your knitting with you. You start each square with the longest row. As you knit, the rows get shorter, and your knitting goes faster until there are no stitches left to bind off.

Materials

Yarn: bulky yarn in assorted colors of your choice, 2,450yd/2,240m

Note: Each square uses approximately 70yd/64m. You can make all of the squares in one color, make each strip a different color, or arrange the colors randomly as I did.

Knitting needles: 5.5mm (size 9 U.S.) circular needles 51cm/20" or longer *or size to obtain gauge*

200yd/183m neutral colored 4 medium weight cotton yarn for sewing seams

Tapestry needle for weaving in ends and sewing seams

2 yd/2m of cotton or cotton-poly blend fabric, 45"/114cm wide, and matching sewing thread for lining

Sewing needle for attaching lining

Gauge

For this rug, make the first square as your gauge swatch. If you don't like the feel of the fabric or the size of the square, you haven't wasted much time. But if you do like the way the swatch comes out, you are already finished with your first square!

One square = 9"/23cm as knit

12 sts and 24 rows = 4"/10cm over Garter st

Always take time to check your gauge.

Size

Approx 45 x 63"/114 x 160cm after sewing and lining

Pattern Stitch

Garter Stitch

Knit every stitch in every row.

Instructions

Note: If you use the same yarn I did, each ball makes one square.

Mitered Square (make 35)

1. Cast on 55 stitches.

2. Worked double-decrease pattern:

Row 1 (RS): k26 st, sl2, k1, p2sso, k26.

See page 35 for slip two, knit one, pass slipped stitches over (sl2, k1, p2sso) double-decrease instructions.

Row 2 and all even (WS) rows: knit all stitches.
Row 3: k25, sl2, k1, p2sso, k25.
Row 5: k24, sl2, k1, p2sso, k24.
Row 7: K23, sl2, k1, p2sso, k23.

Continue working in Garter st, knitting 1 st less before and after the center sl2, k1, p2sso on each RS row.

3. When you have 1 st left, fasten off.

Finishing

Weave in ends.

Note: This yarn frays very easily. Weave in the ends, leaving a tail 2"/5cm long. Tie an overhand knot in the tail to keep it from unweaving itself. These will be hidden inside the lining.

To avoid having bulky seams from this heavy cotton yarn, use a 4 medium weight cotton yarn to sew the squares together on the wrong side. Make five strips of seven squares each, then sew the strips together.

Garter st lies flat, so blocking is optional.

Attach the lining. See Finishing Techniques for instructions on sewing seams on (page 50) and lining rugs (page 53).

This rug was knit with
Artful Yarns' *Dance*, 100% cotton, 70yd/64m per skein, 35 skeins in assorted colors.

4 skeins each:
(A) Tango #916
(B) Fox Trot #914
(C) Highland Fling #911
(D) Polka #913
(E) Macarena #903

5 skeins each:
(F) Jig #908
(G) Jitterbug #907
(H) Hustle #912

Design Tip

I made my rug in five strips of seven squares each. For a smaller rug, make fewer squares. For a larger rug, make more. Because each ball of the yarn I used makes one square, figuring out how much yarn you need is easy.

knit-and-purl rugs

After you've learned to purl, you'll want some practice. Combining knits and purls together creates more options for interesting designs. The rugs in this section include several pattern stitches that are perfect for beginning knitters. These rugs also make great mindless knitting projects for more advanced knitters because the pattern stitches are easily memorized.

Knit and purls combined into smooth stockinette stitch make great practice fabric because you knit all of the stitches on the right side and purl on the wrong side. Different combinations of knits and purls produce an infinite variety of textures and let you practice switching back and forth between knits and purls in the same row. While not all knit-and-purl stitch patterns are reversible, several of the rugs in this section use stitches that are the same on the right and wrong sides.

Knit-and-Purl Hearth Rug

This oval design was inspired by Early American braided rugs. Made from old rags, these early rugs represent frugality and parsimony, but their flamboyant colors speak of a love of beauty. This rug, made of alternating Garter and Stockinette Stitch strips, gives you the chance to bring the classic braided look into your own home.

Finished Measurements
Approx 24 x 36"/61 x 91cm

Materials
Yarn: super bulky wool yarn

Color A (charcoal), 132 yd/121m
Color B (red), 264 yd/241m
Color C (light gray), 264 yd/241m

Knitting needles: 7mm (size 10½ U.S.) straight or double-pointed needles, or size to obtain gauge

Medium weight yarn in a matching color for sewing seams (optional)

Tapestry needle to weave in ends and sew strips together

Gauge
8 st strip = 3"/7.5cm wide as knit over Garter st

Always take time to check your gauge.

Note: Garter st and St st work up at different gauges using the same yarn and needles, but the difference is negligible on these narrow 8-st strips.

Pattern Stitches
Garter Stitch

Knit every stitch in every row.

Stockinette Stitch

Row 1 and all RS rows: knit all stitches.
Row 2 and all WS rows: purl all stitches.

Repeat rows 1 and 2 for pattern.

Instructions

This rug is worked with a center strip and four oval strips sewn together. To easily measure and make sure each strip is the right size, block the strips, and sew them on as you complete each one.

Center
1. With color A (charcoal) cast on 3 sts. Work in Garter st.

2. Increase every row as follows until you have 8 sts: K1, m1, k to end of row, turn.

3. Work even on 8 st for 14"/36cm.

4. Decrease every row as follows until only 3 sts remain: K1, k2tog, k to end of row, turn.

5. Bind off.

Strip 1
1. With color B (red), cast on 8 sts. Work in St st.

2. Work even for 6"/15cm.

3. Work curve with short rows as follows:

Note: Each line in the following instructions tells you what to do on two rows of knitting. Sometimes you turn in the middle of the row, instead of working all 8 sts. This technique is called a "short row." When you work a short row in St st, you must "wrap-and-turn" (w&t) or there will be a hole in the knitting. For instructions on working short rows with the wrap-and-turn technique, see pages 36-37.

Rows 1 (RS) and 2 (WS): K7 w&t, p7 turn
Rows 3 and 4: k8 turn, p8 turn
Rows 5 and 6: K7 w&t, p7 turn
Rows 7 and 8: k8 turn, p8 turn
Rows 9 and 10: K6 w&t, p6 turn
Rows 11 and 12: k8 turn, p8 turn
Rows 13 and 14: k8 turn, p8 turn
Rows 15 and 16: K4 w&t, p4 turn
Rows 17 and 18: k8 turn, p8 turn
Rows 19 and 20: K3 w&t, p3 turn
Rows 21 and 22: k8 turn, p8 turn
Rows 23 and 24: K3 w&t, p3 turn
Rows 25 and 26: k8 turn, p8 turn
Rows 27 and 28: K4 w&t, p4 turn
Rows 29 and 30: k8 turn, p8 turn
Rows 31 and 32: K5 w&t, p5 turn
Rows 33 and 34: k8 turn, p8 turn
Rows 35 and 36: K6 w&t, p6 turn
Rows 37 and 38: k8 turn, p8 turn
Rows 39 and 40: K7 w&t, p7 turn
Rows 41 and 42: k8 turn, p8 turn
Rows 43 and 44: K7 w&t, p7 turn
Rows 45 and 46: k8 turn, p8 turn

4. Work even for 12"/30cm.

5. Work curve as above.

6. Knit even for 6"/15cm.

7. Bind off and sew oval together end to end. Sew to center using whipstitch on WS (see page 50 in Finishing Techniques for instructions on sewing seams).

Note: This yarn is very loosely spun and will fray easily. Use short lengths to sew the strips end to end, and use a stronger medium weight yarn in a matching color to sew seams.

Strip 2
1. With color C (light gray), cast on 8 sts. Work in Garter st.

2. Knit even for 6"/15cm.c.

3. Work curve with short rows as follows:

Rows 1 and 2: K8 turn, k8 turn
Rows 3 and 4: K8 turn, k8 turn
Rows 5 and 6: K6 w&t, k6 turn
Repeat rows 1-6 23 times.

4. Knit even for 12"/30cm.

5. Work curve as above.

6. Knit even for 6"/15cm.

7. Bind off and sew oval together end to end. Sew to previous strip using whipstitch on WS.

Strip 3
1. With color B (red), cast on 8 sts. Work in St st.

2. Work even for 6"/15cm.

Design Tip

Combine three strands of medium weight yarn for a cool-weather tweedy look.

2. Work even for 6"/15cm.

3. Work curve with short rows as follows:

Rows 1 (RS) and 2 (WS): K8 turn, p8 turn
Rows 3 and 4: K8 turn, p8 turn
Rows 5 and 6: K6 w&t, p6 turn
Repeat rows 1-6 23 times.

4. Work even for 12"/30cm.

5. Work curve as above.

6. Work even for 6"/15cm.

7. Bind off and sew oval together end to end. Sew to previous strip using whipstitch on WS.

Strip 4

1. With color A (charcoal), cast on 8 sts. Work in Garter st.

2. Work even in the following stripe pattern until the strip reaches completely around the outer edge of rug:

Color A (charcoal), 8 rows
Color C (light gray), 4 rows
Color A (charcoal), 8 rows
Color C (light gray), 4 rows
Color A (charcoal), 2 rows
Color C (light gray), 4 rows

3. Bind off and sew oval together end to end. Sew to previous strip using whipstitch on WS.

Finishing

Weave in the ends and block, if desired.

This rug was knit with
Brown Sheep's *Burly Spun*, 100% wool, 132yd/121m per skein:

(A) 1 skein, Deep Charcoal #006
(B) 2 skeins, Ruby Red #180
(C) 2 skeins, Gray Heather #003

HISTORICAL TECHNIQUE
Traditional versions of this rug, like the Amish rugs from the early 1900s, did not require short-row shaping. To make an Amish-style rug, make all of the strips from Garter Stitch. Knit each strip until it is long enough to reach around the previous section. The strips will stretch and fit around the oval with no shaping at all. Change colors randomly for a traditional hit-or-miss design, or create your own color pattern as you go.

Country Kitchen Moss Stitch

Because Moss Stitch is so easy, it's a terrific introduction to knit-and-purl stitch patterns. After a few rows, you'll have the motions memorized—you can sit back and enjoy watching the variegated yarn paint a picture as you knit. Embellish your rug with a crochet edge and brushed fringe, as I did, or use your own favorite edging.

Finished Measurements
Approx 24 x 33"/61 x 84cm blocked, without crochet edging and fringe

Materials
Yarn: Any bulky yarn or combination of yarns that gives you the correct gauge, 500yds/457m

Knitting needles: 10mm (size 15 U.S.), 73.5cm/29" long or size to obtain gauge

Blunt tapestry needle for weaving in ends and attaching fringe

6mm (size J U.S.) crochet hook for adding edging

Gauge
9 sts and 14 rows = 4"/10cm over Moss st as knit

Always take time to check your gauge.

Pattern Stitch
Moss Stitch

Row 1 (RS): (K1, p1), repeat to end of row.
Rows 2 and 4 (WS): Knit the knits and purl the purls. See making a Stockinette Stitch Swatch on page 29.
Row 3: (P1, k1), repeat to end of row.

Repeat rows 1-4 for pattern.

Instructions
1. Cast on 54 sts.

2. Work in Moss st for 33"/84cm.

3. Bind off.

Finishing

Add single-crochet edging to the sides of the rug. (For instructions on single crochet, see page 44 in Embellishment & Accessories.

Weave in the ends, block, and let dry.

Attach brushed fringe trim. (For instructions on making fringe, see page 46.)

This rug was knit with
9 skeins of Classic Elite's *Weekend Cotton*, 100% cotton, 51yd/47m per ball, color 4806.

Design Tip
Choose sturdy, resilient yarn if you'll be using this rug in a traffic area. Any color will look good, but variegated and hand-painted yarns add interest to the simple stitch pattern. For a simple, clean design, knit this rug with a solid color or a heathery tweed.

Coiled Cord Oval

This oval rug can be knit using double-pointed needles or a knitting knobby spool. The easy, repetitive stitch is an ideal relaxation technique to use while you're commuting on the subway, waiting in the doctor's office, or even while you're watching TV. It's also a great way to teach your children how to knit.

Finished Measurements
Approx 24 x 36"/61 x 91cm after sewing and blocking

Materials
Yarn: bulky yarn in wool or wool blend

    Color A (taupe), 545yd/498m
    Color B (brown), 545yd/498m

Knitting needles: Two 6mm (size 10 U.S.) double-pointed needles

Tapestry needle to weave in ends and sew cord into oval

Gauge
4 st cord = approx ½"/1.5cm wide as knit

Pattern Stitch
Knitted cord

Row 1 (and all rows): Knit all stitches. Do not turn. Slide the stitches to opposite end of the double-pointed needle.

Repeat row 1 for pattern stitch.

Instructions

1. Cast on 4 st with color A (taupe).

2. Work 4 st knitted cord, changing colors as desired. Measuring the progress of knitted cord with a ruler can be arduous. Instead, change colors whenever you use up a couple of balls of yarn:

2½ balls color A (taupe)
2 balls color B (brown)
2 balls color A (taupe)
2½ balls color B (brown)

Note: To make this project more portable, work each ball (or half-ball) of yarn as a separate piece of knitted cord, and sew them together end to end before assembling into the oval.

3. Bind off.

Finishing

On the WS, whipstitch cord into oval, being careful not to let cord twist. See page 50 in Finishing Touches for instructions on sewing seams.

Note: If your yarn frays, use a sturdier yarn in a matching color for sewing seams.

This rug was knit with
Reynolds' *Lopi*, 100% Icelandic wool, 109yd/100m, 3.5oz/100g per ball

5 balls each:
(A) Taupe #367
(B) Heather Brown #452

For a different texture, many 19th-century knitters made this style of rug using strips of Stockinette st or Garter st instead of knitted cord. Cast on 7 or 8 sts with medium weight yarn, and knit away. If you slip the first stitch of every row, you'll have a nice smooth edge for sewing the strips together. You can change colors randomly, and coil the strips in hit-or-miss fashion, or make each strip from a single color, and arrange them in concentric circles.

Design Tip

This rug can be made in virtually any yarn, at any gauge. Even lightweight yarns will work up into a thick rug because of the shape of the knitted cord. I used 100 percent wool yarn in a bulky weight to make the knitting go quickly.

Welcome guests to your home with this eco-chic knit-and-purl doormat, made with strong-as-rope hemp yarn. In its natural color, hemp beautifully shows off this distinctive checkerboard pattern. Knit the mat in a rich, earthy color if you have lots of little feet or paws tracking in mud.

Hemp Doormat

Finished Measurements

Approx 27 x 18"/69 x 46cm blocked

Materials

Yarn: medium weight yarn made from any sturdy, hard-wearing fiber such as cotton or hemp, 750yds/686m

Knitting needles: 5mm (size 8 U.S) circular needle, 80cm/32" long *or size to obtain gauge*

Note: Because the hemp yarn I used is fairly stiff to work with, dropped stitches simply refuse to unravel. A quick-knitting nickel-plated needle will let the yarn slide along with ease.

Blunt tapestry needle to weave in ends

Gauge

14 sts and 18 rows = 4"/10cm blocked, over Checkerboard st. Be sure you wash and press your swatch before measuring because the hemp yarn relaxes when it's washed.

Always take time to check your gauge.

Pattern Stitches

Garter Stitch

Knit every stitch of every row.

Checkerboard Stitch

Rows 1-8:
RS rows: p8, k8.
WS rows: Making a Stockinette Stitch Swatch on page 29.

Rows 9-16:
RS rows: k8, p8.
WS rows: knit the knits and purl the purls.

Repeat rows 1-16 for pattern.

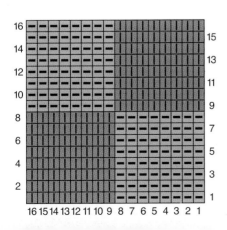

16 15 14 13 12 11 10 9 8 7 6 5 4 3 2 1

Instructions

1. Using a double strand of yarn, cast on 88 sts.

2. Work 7 rows of Garter st. End with a WS row.

3. Begin Checkerboard st with Garter st border.

Setup row (RS):
K4 (Garter st border).
Place marker (pm), work Checkerboard st to last 4 sts, pm.
K4 (Garter st border).

Work pattern stitches as established, slipping markers when you come to them.

Repeat rows 1-16 of Checkerboard st chart 3 times.

Repeat rows 1-8 once more.

End with a WS row.

4. Work 7 rows of Garter st.

5. Bind off.

Finishing

Weave in the ends.

You'll notice that your rug looks more like a miniature hilly landscape than a beautiful doormat. Don't panic. Blocking the rug will relax the fibers and flatten it out.

Wash this rug to block it. Hemp can be washed by hand or gently machine washed (see washing instructions on page 54 in Finishing Touches). The hemp softens with each washing, without weakening the fibers. For other yarns, follow manufacturer's washing instructions. Lay the rug on a flat surface and press it firmly with lots of steam. Leave it to dry.

Working with hemp yarn can be hard on your hands if you try to knit too tightly. Knit at a gauge that is comfortable for you. Because the hemp is so strong, it's okay if your stitches seem a little loose. If you use a cotton yarn, make sure the stitches are firm so the rug will keep its shape and hold up to wear.

This rug was knit with
4 skeins of Lana Knits' *HH-12*, 100% Hemp, 190 yd/174m per skein, Natural

pile rugs

According to Lydia LeBaron Walker, author of *Homecraft Rugs*, which she wrote in 1929, pile rugs are the "patricians" of hand-knit rugs. Today, many people are unaware that it's possible—and easy—to knit shaggy pile rugs. Made on basic Garter Stitch or Stockinette Stitch backgrounds, they are among the simplest rugs to knit. The rugs in this section use four unusual pile-knitting techniques. Each creates a thick and plush rug with a unique texture.

To make *knit-in pile*, pre-cut strips of yarn are inserted between knitted stitches and pushed to the front of the work to create a built-in furry surface. To knit *loopy pile*, the same yarn is used for the backing and loops, so there's no need to keep track of two separate yarns. To make *washboard pile*, long, narrow strips of garter stitch are knit and then sewn onto a fabric backing. To add *afterthought pile*, strips are cut and then added to the surface of the work with a crochet hook, like fringe or latch-hook pile, after the knitting is completed.

Knit-and-Sew Washboard Runner

I discovered this unusual knit-and-sew technique in a 1929 knitting book. Knit from strips of Garter Stitch that are then folded in half and sewn onto a fabric background, the resulting texture resembles an old-fashioned washboard. It's thick, but soft, making it equally suited to protect traffic areas or warm toes at bedside.

Finished Measurements
18 x 48"/46 x 122cm after sewing

Materials
Yarn: medium weight yarn

Color A (pink), 200yd/183m
Color B (mauve), 400yd/366m
Color C (plum), 800yd/732m

Knitting needles: 4.5mm (size 7 U.S.) circular needle 24"/61cm or longer or size to obtain gauge

Tapestry needle to weave in ends

1½yd/1.5m pillow ticking or other striped cotton fabric 45"/114cm wide

Sewing thread and sewing needle for sewing strips to backing and attaching non-stick lining

Gauge
6 st strip = 1½"/4cm wide over Garter st

Always take time to check your gauge.

Pattern Stitch

Garter Stitch

Knit every stitch in every row.

Instructions

Strips
Make 28:

4 with color A
8 with color B
16 with color C

1. Cast on 6 sts.

2. Work in Garter st for 48"/122cm.

3. Bind off.

Finishing

Fold the strips in half lengthwise and whipstitch them to the backing approx ⅜"/1cm apart. Use the lines on the preshrunk pillow ticking as a guide to keep them straight.

Note: If your strips are not all exactly the same length, don't worry. You can easily stretch the Garter st strip to fit as you sew it on the backing.

Run the ends inside the tubes formed by sewing the strips onto the backing.

Sew on non-slip backing if desired.

This rug was knit with
Plymouth's Encore Worsted, 75% Acrylic, 25% Wool, 200yd/183m, 3.5oz/100g per ball

(A) 1 ball, Pink #241
(B) 2 balls, Mauve #433
(C) 4 balls, Plum #355

HISTORICAL TECHNIQUE
In the early 20th century, washboard rugs were made in many different shapes. Here's how one knitter described her knit-and-sew technique to make a circular pattern:

Put a jumbo-sized thumb tack in the middle of your backing fabric and attach a string with a pencil tied onto the other end. Go around and around with the pencil, drawing a coil on the fabric as you go. As the string wraps around the tack, the coil will get smaller. Use this line to sew your strips to the backing in a snail-shell pattern.

Design Tip

This rug can be made with any medium weight yarn. If you want a stronger rug to use as a doormat, use cotton or hemp to create a firm, stiff mat. If you want a soft rug to use as a bath mat, use wool or chenille to create a plush texture.

Berber Rya

My friends are always surprised that shag rugs can be knitted. Snippets of yarn laid in between the knit stitches create the fluffy texture of a retro shag rug from the 1960s or a Norse rya from a thousand years earlier. Because the background stitch is hidden by the shag, I used Garter Stitch so you never have to purl.

Finished Measurements
Approx. 24 x 36"/61 x 91cm including single-crochet border

Materials
Yarn: This rug uses two yarns, one for the knit backing and a second for the pile

For knitting, medium weight cotton yarn, 800yd/732m

For pile and edging, super bulky wool rug yarn, 800yd/732m

Knitting needles: 4.5mm (size 7 U.S.) circular needle at least 61cm/24" long *or size to obtain gauge*

Tapestry needle to weave in ends

Paint-on liquid latex rug backing

Gauge
11 sts and 24 rows = 4"/10cm measured on WS over Pile st

Always take time to check your gauge.

Pattern Note
Reserve 65yd/59m of pile yarn for single-crochet edging

Pattern Stitch
Pile Stitch

The pile, or shag, is added on wrong side rows on an odd number of stitches. For instructions on knitting-in pile, see page 37 in Special Techniques.

Row 1 and all right side (RS) rows: Knit.
Row 2 and all wrong side (WS) rows: (K1, insert two strands of pile yarn, k1, fold pile strands over new stitch to RS of work.) Repeat to last st. k1.

Repeat rows 1 and 2 for pattern. End on a RS row.

Instructions

Cut pile yarn into 4"/10cm pieces.

Make four pieces (with all of the pile yarn attached to the backing, this rug is much too heavy to knit in one piece):

1. Cast on 61 sts with knitting yarn.

2. Work in Pile st until piece measures 8"/20 cm.

3. Bind off.

Finishing

Sew four pieces together using whipstitch on WS. For instructions on sewing seams, see page 50 in Finishing Touches.

Work single-crochet edging around entire rug using pile yarn. Work 3 single-crochets in each corner st. For instructions on crocheting edgings, see page 44 in Embellishments & Accessories.

Weave in the ends.

Paint on liquid latex backing, following manufacturer's directions, to lock in pile (see page 52 in Finishing Touches).

This rug was knit with
Knitting yarn: 2 balls Aunt Lydia's *Denim Quick Crochet,* 75% cotton/25% acrylic, 400yd/366m per ball, Milk #1002

Pile and edging yarn: 12 skeins Halcyon Yarn's, *Halcyon Rug Wool,* 100% wool, 65yd/59m, 4oz/113g per skein, color 131

HISTORICAL TECHNIQUE
If you'd like to knit a pile rug with fabric strips for the shaggy surface, follow these instructions I found in an 1854 edition of *Godey's Lady's Book*—**although more than 150 years old, these instructions are still valid for today's knitters:** "Hearth rugs are sometimes made by cutting cloth into strips ½" (1.5 cm) wide and 2" (5cm) long, and knitting them together with string. This is done by inserting the piece of cloth exactly at the middle, in the loop of the knitting, and drawing it very tight; it is rather hard finger-work, and some make the rug by sewing the strips of cloth on to a piece of old carpet or any other strong material that may be at hand."

Rag Rug Technique

Try using strips of fabric for the pile instead of yarn. Quilting cotton, T-shirt knits, or fleece would all create interesting textures.

Toe-Cozy Bath Mat

You'll want to take a shower just so you can snuggle your toes in the furry fabric of this loopy pile bath mat. The background fabric is Garter Stitch, so if you're a new knitter you don't have to worry about purling; the Loop Stitch keeps the project interesting if you're a more advanced knitter.

Finished Measurements
Approx. 20 x 28"/51 x 71cm, blocked

Materials
Yarn: medium weight unmercerized cotton, 1100 yds/1005m

Knitting Needles: 5.5mm (size 9 U.S.) circular needle 60cm/24" or longer, or size to obtain gauge

Note: I usually recommend wooden needles for cotton, but the Loop Stitch can be difficult to get used to, and I found that a slick metal needle made the work go faster without cramping up my hands.

Blunt tapestry needle for weaving in ends

Gauge
12 sts and 20 rows = 4"/10cm over Loop st

Always take time to check your gauge.

The gauge of Loop st is difficult to measure because the loops hide the knitting stitches on the right side. To make a practice swatch of Loop st:

1. Cast on 20 stitches, and work 8 rows of Garter st.

2. Set up Loop st, and work in pattern for 20 rows.

3. Work 8 rows Garter st and bind off.

Measure your gauge on the wrong side in the Loop st area, between the Garter st borders:

☞ If the Loop st section measures less than 4"/10cm, switch to a larger size needle.

☞ If the Loop st section measures more than 4"/10cm, switch to a smaller size needle.

Note: If you like the fabric even if your gauge is off, just knit the rug. Depending on your gauge, it will come out larger or smaller than the one I made.

Pattern Stitches
Garter Stitch

Knit every stitch in every row.

Loop Stitch

For detailed instructions on making loops, see page 38 in Special Techniques.

Row 1 and 3 (RS): knit all sts.
Row 2 (WS): (k1, make loop), repeat across Loop st section.
Row 4 (WS): (make loop, k1), repeat across Loop st section.
Repeat rows 1-4 for stitch pattern.

Note: As you get started, you may feel clumsy trying to make the loops, but after a bit of practice you'll develop your own rhythm.

Instructions

1. Cast on 36 sts using a double strand of yarn.

2. Work 8 rows of Garter st, inc 1 st at the beginning of every row until you have 44 sts as follows:

K4, m1, k to end of row.

(For instructions on the m1 increase, see page 34.)

Today, Loop Stitch is worked with one yarn, whereas the Loop Stitch popular in the early 20th century used a strong, cotton string for the knitting and a plush yarn for the pile, making it perfectly suited for rugs. Instructions of the day went something like this: Insert the needle into the next stitch. Wind the pile yarn around the needle as if to make a stitch and around two fingers of the left hand. Bring the knitting yarn over the needle and complete the stitch, including the pile strands in it. On plain rows, include the pile strands in each stitch.

Design Tip

Unmercerized cotton is the most popular yarn for kitchen and bathroom projects because it's softer and more absorbent than mercerized cotton. It's also practical because you can toss it right into the washer and dryer. But cotton is not the only choice you have. Wool rugs can hold up to 30 percent of their weight in water without feeling wet or cold to your feet. If you find that knitting the Loop Stitch in cotton yarn puts too much stress on your hands, make the rug with a washable wool yarn. The natural give of the wool is easier on the fingers for many knitters.

3. Begin Loop st with 4 st Garter st border.

Set up row (RS):

K4 (Garter st border).
Place marker (pm), work Loop st to last 4 sts, pm.
K4 (Garter st border).

4. Work increase section.

Row 1 and all WS rows: K4 (Garter st border), slip marker (sm), m1, work Loop st to second marker, sm, k4 (Garter st border).

Row 2 and all RS rows: K4, sm, m1, k to end of row, slipping second marker when you come to it.

Note: As you increase, don't forget to offset the loops on every other loop row.

Continue increasing until you have 54 sts.

5. Work even in pattern stitches as established, slipping markers when you come to them, until rug is 24.5"/60cm.

6. Work decrease section.

(For instructions on the k2tog decrease, see page 35 in Special Techniques.)

Row 1 and all WS rows: K4 (Garter st border), sm, k2tog, work Loop st until second marker, sm, k4 (Garter st border).

RS rows: K4, sm, k2tog, knit to end of row, slipping second marker when you come to it.

Continue decreasing until 44 sts remain.
Remove markers.

7. Work eight rows of Garter st, decreasing 1 st at the beginning of every row as follows:

K4, k2tog, knit to end of row.

8. BO remaining 36 sts.

Finishing

Weave in the ends.

If desired, apply paint-on latex backing to lock in loops.

This rug was knit with
5 balls, Lion Brand's, *Lion Cotton*, 100% cotton, 236yd/216m, Cinnamon #135

Waterfall Fringe

When I showed this rug to a friend, she exclaimed, "It's a beautiful waterfall!" and so it was named. The Stockinette Stitch background is made with a double strand of yarn that changes slowly from light blue to navy, creating a subtle blended effect, like the reflection of an autumn sky on a lake. To make the project go faster, you "latch hook" the shaggy pile after you're finished knitting.

Finished Measurements
Approx 30 x 46"/76 x 117cm blocked, without fringe

Materials
Yarn: This rug uses two yarns, one for the knit backing and a second for the pile

For knitting, medium weight wool yarn (used double), 920yds/841m

For pile and fringe, medium weight wool yarn in coordinating color, 920yds/841m

Knitting needles: 6mm (size 11 U.S.) circular needle 74cm/29" or longer, or size to obtain gauge

Blunt tapestry needle to weave in ends

Row counter

Crochet hook to attach fringe and pile

Gauge
Approx 9 sts and 13 rows = 4"/10cm over St st blocked

Always take time to check your gauge.

Pattern Stitch
Stockinette Stitch

Row 1 and all RS rows: knit all stitches.
Row 2 and all WS rows: purl all stitches.
Repeat rows 1 and 2 for pattern.

Instructions

1. With a double strand of color A (#9) cast on 30 sts. Working in St st, follow this color sequence for the whole rug:

AA Two strands of A 20 rows
AB One strand of A and B 10 rows
BB Two strands of B 10 rows
BC One strand of B and C 8 rows
CC Two strands of C 8 rows
CD One strand of C and D 8 rows
DD Two strands of D 24 rows
DE One strand of D and E 8 rows
EE Two strands of E 8 rows
EF One strand of E and F 8 rows
FF Two strands of F 10 rows
FG One strand of F and G 10 rows
GG Two strands of G 20 rows

2. Work increase section:

Row 1 (RS): k1, m1, k to last st, m1, k1.
Row 2 (WS): purl all stitches.
Repeat Rows 1 and 2 until you have 72 sts.

For instructions on the m1 increase, see page 34.

3. Work even in St st until rug measures approx. 34"/86cm and you are on row 2 of color FF (#13).

4. Work decrease section:

Row 1 (RS): k2tog, k to last 2 st, k2tog.
Row 2 (WS): purl all stitches.
Repeat Rows 1 and 2 until 30 sts remain.

For instructions on the k2tog decrease, see page 35.

5. Bind off.

Finishing

Weave in the ends. Block to uncurl Stockinette st edges.

Add fringe around edge of rug, reversing color sequence. See page 46 in Embellishments & Accessories for instructions on making fringe.

Add the latch-hook design, reversing color sequence and following chart for placement of pile:

1. Cut yarn for pile in 3"/7.5cm lengths.

2. Place the rug on a flat surface, with the RS facing up.

3. Attach the pile as you would if it were fringe, but to the surface of the knitting instead of to the edge:

Insert a crochet hook under a bar between two columns of knit stitches, and back to the front of the work.

Wrap two pieces of yarn around the crochet hook, and draw a loop through.

Draw the ends of the pile yarn through the loop, and tug gently to secure. Work loosely so you don't distort the knitted fabric.

4. Fluff the pile with your fingers.

Note: Follow the outline of the design, then fill in the center of each ray, attaching one double strand of pile every other stitch. Don't worry about being exact. If you fudge and skip a stitch every now and then, it won't show.

This rug was knit with
Halcyon Yarn's:

Geo Rug Wool, 100% wool, 115 yds/105m per skein (Rug Body)

(A) Color # 9, 1 skein
(B) Color # 10, 1 skein
(C) Color # 15, 1 skein
(D) Color # 11, 2 skeins
(E) Color # 14, 1 skein
(F) Color # 13, 1 skein
(G) Color # 12, 1 skein

Deco Rug Wool, 100% wool, 115 yds/105m per skein (Pile and Fringe)

(A) Color # 9, 1 skein
(B) Color # 10, 1 skein
(C) Color # 15, 1 skein
(D) Color # 11, 2 skeins
(E) Color # 14, 1 skein
(F) Color # 13, 1 skein
(G) Color # 12, 1 skein

Note: Colors are listed light to dark.

Design Tip

You can work the entire rug in one color, the rug body in one color and the fringe and pile in a coordinating tone, or create a blend of tones in one family as I've done. I combined two yarns with slight nuances in color and texture to create a smooth blending of colors. I knit the rug using a singles yarn that is similar in size and color to the plied yarn that I used for the fringe and pile. Both yarns are dyed together to produce tone variations in the same shades. Because the singles yarn is dyed on natural heathered gray wool, its rich colors have an earthy and homespun appeal.

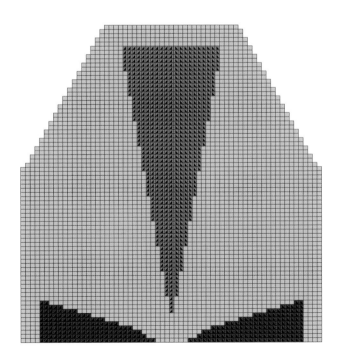

color-work rugs

Color is the first thing most people see when flipping through a catalog or looking for an item to decorate their home. There are several different techniques for combining colors in knitting. Not all of the rugs in the other sections of this book are monochrome. But when they do contain multiple colors, they're added one at a time in separate blocks or stripes. The rugs in this section, in contrast, are made by using two colors on the same row of knitting.

Intarsia is a method of knitting that lets you add blocks of color right in the middle of a solid background. These blocks can be large geometric shapes, or small delicate details like the petals of a flower.

Stranded knitting, sometimes called *Fair Isle*, is used for all-over two-color patterns that are often seen in ethnic designs. These patterns are easiest worked "in-the-round" so you don't have to struggle with purling two yarns at once.

Mosaic or *slipstitch knitting* mimics stranded knitting by having two colors on the same row, but you only knit with one color at a time. You "slip" stitches of the second color from the previous row to make them magically appear to be where they are not.

Crayon Color-Block Sampler

Who says your knitting has to "stay in the lines"? This rug starts off with basic Garter Stitch, but changes to a different color and stitch pattern in each section. The crayon shades of the heavy-duty rug wool create a fun geometric design that adds spark to any child's room.

Finished Measurements
Approx 30 x 42"/76 x 107cm, blocked

Materials

Yarn: super bulky rug wool

> Color A (fuchsia), 195yd/178m
> Color B (yellow), 195yd/178m
> Color C (light teal), 130yd/119m
> Color D (orange), 195yd/178m
> Color E (dark teal), 130yd/119m

Knitting needles: 12mm (size 17 U.S.) circular needle at least 74cm/29" long, or *size to obtain gauge*

Blunt tapestry needle for weaving in ends

Gauge
Approx 6 sts and 9 rows = 4"/10cm over Seed st

Always take time to check your gauge.

Note: Work a large enough swatch to include several rows of each stitch pattern, and to make sure your hands are comfortable working with the double strand of super bulky yarn on the size needles you've chosen. If you work too tightly, you may find that your hands cramp up. Because each stitch pattern works up to a slightly different gauge, make sure you like the texture and density of your gauge swatch.

Pattern Notes
This rug is knit with a double strand of yarn.

When changing to a new color, always start on the right side and knit all stitches of the new color. When you purl in a new color, it pulls a loop of the old color up into the new row and makes a bump, interrupting the straight line of the color change. All of the stitch patterns for this rug start with a WS row, so the color change will be an all-knit RS row.

Pattern Stitches
Garter Stitch

Knit every stitch of every row.

Small Checkerboard Stitch

Row 1 (WS): K2, p2. Repeat to end of row.
Rows 2 and 4 (RS): Knit the knits and purl the purls.
Row 3: P2, k2. Repeat to end of row.

Repeat rows 1-4 for pattern

Moss Stitch

Row 1 (WS): K1, p1. Repeat to end of row.
Rows 2 and 4 (RS): Knit the knits and purl the purls.
Row 3: P1, k1. Repeat to end of row.

Repeat rows 1-4 for pattern.

Seed Stitch

Row 1 (WS): K1, p1. Repeat to end of row.
Row 2 (RS): Purl the knits and knit the purls.

Repeat rows 1 and 2 for pattern.

This rug can be made in any super bulky wool yarn. Each stitch pattern works up at a slightly different gauge and weight, so wool is the best choice because it's so pliable when wet, making it easy to block the rug to even out the texture. Pastels are perfect for a new baby's room, while bright primaries are more exciting for an active preschooler. A subtle neutral palette is ideal for the grown-ups' areas of the house.

Reverse Sand Stitch

Row 1 (WS): K1, p1. Repeat to end of row.
Row 2 (RS): Knit all stitches.

Repeat rows 1 and 2 for pattern.

Instructions

1. With a double strand of color A (fucshia), cast on 50 sts.

2. Work in Garter st for 10"/25 cm. End on a WS row.

3. Begin yellow and light teal color blocks. Starting on a RS row, k 28 sts with color B (yellow), then 22 sts with color C (light teal).

Work stitch patterns as follows:

Work 22 sts in color C (light teal) in Moss st.

Work 28 sts color B (yellow) in small Checkerboard st.

Note: Twist yarns when changing colors. For instructions, see Intarsia Color Knitting on pages 39-40 in Special Techniques.

Work even until color C (light teal) measures 12"/30cm. End with a WS row.

4. Begin orange color block. Starting on a RS row, work 28 stitches with color B (yellow). Cut C (light teal), and knit the remaining 22 sts with color D (orange).

Work stitch patterns as follows:

Work 22 sts in color D (orange) in Reverse Sand st. Work 28 sts in color B (yellow) in small Checkerboard st.

Work even in patterns until color B (yellow) measures 24"/61cm. End with a WS row.

5. Begin dark teal color block. Cut color B (yellow). Starting on a RS row, k 28 sts using color E (dark teal). Continue working in Reverse Sand st across the remaining 22 sts using color D (orange).

Work stitch patterns as follows:

Work 22 sts in color D (orange) in Reverse Sand st. Work 28 sts in color E (dark teal) in Seed st.

Work even until the color E (dark teal) measures 12"/30cm. End with a WS row.

6. Bind off.

Finishing

Weave in the ends and block.

Because Garter st is denser than the other stitches used in this rug, lightly steam the rug to open up the garter ridges and give the fabric a more consistent weight and texture.

This rug was knit with
Halcyon's *Rug Wool*, 100% Wool, 64yds/59m per skein:

(A) 3 skeins, #176 fuchsia
(B) 3 skeins, #181 yellow
(C) 2 skeins, #183 light teal
(D) 3 skeins, #180 orange
(E) 2 skeins, #182 dark teal

Fair Isle In-the-Round

This rug is knit "in the round"—you join your knitting in a circle, and go around and around, watching a large tube grow on your needles. After you finish knitting, you cut—don't faint!—the tube open, and unravel the edge stitches to magically create the attached fringe. To be true to the Fair Isle knitting tradition and to keep the project simple, I used only two colors in a row.

Design Tips

This rug can be made in any super bulky yarn. Wool is a good choice because it's easy to weave in all of the ends from the different colors without worrying that they will come undone.

For a more formal design, work all of the strips with the same color or with different shades in the same family. To spice things up a bit, choose the shades of cinnamon, saffron, and cayenne, or the bright reds, yellows, and greens of ripe chili peppers.

In color knitting you often have yarn left over. With this project, you should have enough yarn to make the rug plus a few accent pillows. See page 47 in Embellishments & Accessories for pillow instructions.

Finished Measurements

31 x 46"/79 x 117cm, after blocking, not including fringe

Materials

Yarn: 6 super bulky rug wool:

Color A (tan), 130yd/119m
Color B (cream), 320yd/293m
Color C (blue), 130yd/119m
Color D (green), 130yd/119m
Color E (yellow), 130yd/119m
Color F (mauve), 130yd/119m
Color G (lavender), 130yd/119m

Knitting needles: 6mm and 8mm (sizes 10 and 11 U.S.) circular needles 61cm/24" or longer or size to obtain gauge

Sewing shears to cut fringe

Rotary cutter to trim fringe

Large plastic ruler to trim fringe

Tapestry needle to weave in ends

Gauge

11 stitches and 10 rows = 4"/10cm over two-color stranded St st in-the-round

Always take time to check your gauge.

Note: If you don't have short circular needles to knit a gauge swatch, use your longer needles. Knit across one row, then—instead of turning—slide your knitting to the other end of the circular needle, and loosely strand the working yarns across the back. This will give you an accurate gauge sample because you are still knitting every row instead of purling the WS rows.

Pattern Stitches

Stockinette Stitch (in-the-round)

Knit every stitch in every row.

Seed Stitch

Round 1 (WS): K1, p1. Repeat to end of row.
Round 2 (RS): Purl the knits and knit the purls.

Repeat rounds 1 and 2 for pattern.

Instructions

1. With smaller needle and color A (tan), cast on 81 sts.

At the beginning of each round, wrap yarn around the right needle 10 times. When you are working with two colors in a row, wrap both yarns together.

Knit the first and last stitches of each round through the back loop. When you are working with two colors in a row, knit this stitch using both colors together.

Bottom Edge

1. With smaller needle, work four rounds of Seed st.

2. With larger needle, work 3 rounds St st.

3. Add color B (cream) and work rounds 1 and 2 of chart A, rep sts 1-20 four times, then st 21 once more.

Fair Isle strips

1. With larger needle, work strips according to charts. Follow the color sequence below for the background color. In all strips, the pattern color is color B (cream). For each strip, work rows 3-23 of chart, repeating sts 1-20 four times, then st 21 once:

Strip 1—color C (blue), chart A
Strip 2—color D (green), chart B
Strip 3—color E (yellow), chart A
Strip 4—color F (mauve), chart B
Strip 5—color G (lavender), chart A

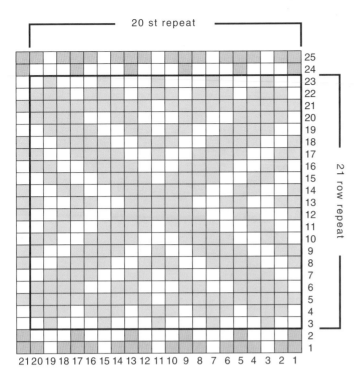

Fair Isle In-the-Round Chart A

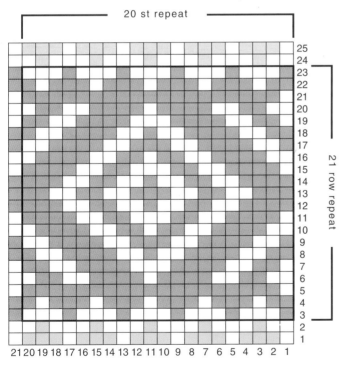

Fair Isle In-the-Round Chart B

Top Edge

1. With colors A (tan) and B (cream), work rounds 24 and 25 or chart A. Cut color B.

2. Work 3 ronds St st.

3. With a smaller needle, work 4 rounds Seed st.

4. Bind off.

Finishing

Cut the rug open in the middle of the fringe. Tie the fringes from each set of two rows in a knot close to the edge of the knitting. Trim the fringes. Weave in the ends and block.

This rug was knit with
Halcyon's Rug Wool, 100% Wool, 64yd/59m per ball.

(A) 2 skeins, #131 tan
(B) 5 skeins, #129 cream
(C) 2 skeins, #142 blue
(D) 2 skeins, #144 green
(E) 2 skeins, #146 yellow
(F) 2 skeins, #140 mauve
(G) 2 skeins, #138 lavender

Thunderbird Intarsia Tapestry

This rug has international roots—knitted Masterpieces made by German knitting guilds as well as Native American tapestries inspired the design. The larger color areas are knit as-you-go, and the smaller motifs are embroidered as a finishing touch.

Finished Measurements
Approx 35 x 44"/89 x 112cm after blocking and lining

Materials
Yarn: bulky weight wool yarn

    Color A (black), 875yd/800m
    Color B (natural), 350yd/320m
    Color C (turquoise), 350yd/320
    Color D (red), 350yd/320m

Knitting Needles: 10mm (size 15 U.S.) circular needle 74cm/29" or longer *or size to obtain gauge*

Tapestry needle to weave in ends

1 yd/1m cotton or cotton-poly blend lining fabric 45"/114cm wide

Sewing thread and sewing needle to attach lining

Dowel or curtain rod to hang

Gauge
Approx 8 sts and 12 rows = 4"/10cm over St st using a double strand of yarn

Always take time to check your gauge

Pattern Stitches
Garter Stitch

Knit every stitch in every row.

Stockinette Stitch

Row 1 and all RS rows: knit all stitches.
Row 2 and all WS rows: purl all stitches.

Repeat rows 1 and 2 for pattern.

Pattern Notes
This rug is knit with a double strand of yarn. This project uses a combination of stranded two-color knitting and intarsia knitting. (See pages 39 to 40 in Special Techniques for instructions.)

The large color areas are knit as you go. Smaller areas, such as the birds' eyes, red stripes, and red dots in the border pattern are embroidered after you finish knitting.

Charts are worked in this order, from bottom to top of rug:

Border
Thunderbird
Left and Right Small Birds
Border

Instructions

Bottom Edge

1. Using a double strand of color A (black), cast on 67 sts.

2. Work six rows of Garter st.

3. Work four rows St st with Garter st borders as follows:

Row 1 (RS): knit all stitches.
Row 2 (WS): k3, place marker (pm), p to last 3 sts, pm, k3.

Repeat rows 1 and 2, slipping markers when you come to them.

Continue in St st with 3 st Garter st border as established for all charts.

Bottom Border Chart

1. Change to color B (natural). Together with color C (turquoise), begin chart in stranded two-color knitting, maintaining 3 st Garter st borders.

Work sts 1-2 once
Repeat sts 3-12 five times
Work sts 13-21 once

Thunderbird Chart

1. Change from color B (natural) to color A (black). Together with Color C (turquoise), work chart in intarsia knitting as follows:

K3 (Garter st border).
Slip marker (sm), K7, pm, work chart, pm, k7, sm.
K3 (Garter st border).

2. Continue in stitch patterns as established, slipping markers whenever you come to them. When chart is complete, break color C (turquoise).

Note: Strand the background color behind the bird's tail and wing feathers.

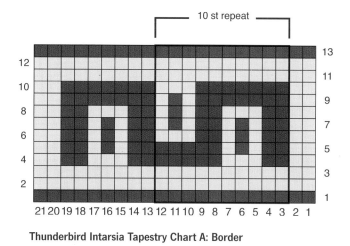

Thunderbird Intarsia Tapestry Chart A: Border

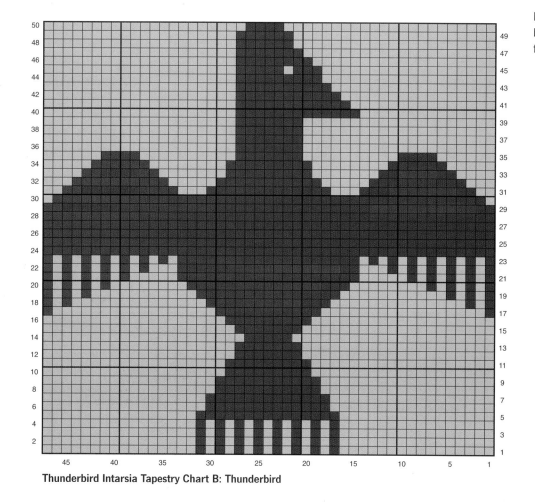

Thunderbird Intarsia Tapestry Chart B: Thunderbird

Left and Right bird charts

Note: Work each small bird with a separate piece of yarn, but strand the background color behind the bird motifs.

1. Continue working with color A (black), and add color D (red).

K3 (Garter st border).
Sm, K3, pm, work Right side Bird chart, pm, k27, pm, work Left side Bird chart, pm, k3, sm.
K3 (Garter st border).

2. Continue in stitch patterns as established, slipping markers whenever you come to them.

Top Border Chart

Work as for bottom border chart.

Bottom Edge

1. Work four rows in 3 st Garter st border pattern as established. Work six rows in Garter st.

2. Bind off.

Finishing

Add embroidery, using the photo as a guide (see Embellishments & Accessories on page 44 for instructions).

Add red horizontal lines using crochet chain stitch.

Work birds' eyes and red dots in the border using duplicate stitch.

Weave in the ends. Wash or steam press to smooth out color work stitches.

Line the rug (see page 53) and add a casing (see page 48) to display it as a wall hanging.

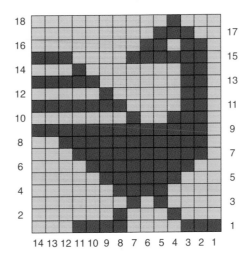

Thunderbird Intarsia Tapestry Chart C: Left side Bird

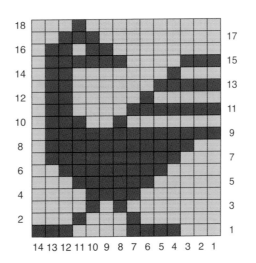

Thunderbird Intarsia Tapestry Chart D: Right side Bird

This rug was knit with
Peace Fleece's *MidEast/Maine Island Yarn*, 100% wool, 175yds/161m, 4oz/125g per skein.

(A) 5 skeins, Silent Night
(B) 2 skeins, Jaffa Beach
(C) 2 skeins, Bedouin Blue
(D) 2 skeins, Red Sea

Mediterranean Mosaic

This tessellating, or repeating, motif was inspired by an intricate tiled floor.
The Mosaic Slipstitch knitting technique makes this runner a great starter
project if you're new to color knitting. You knit with one color in each row,
but it looks as if the colors are intertwined.

Finished Measurements
22 x 44"/56 x 112cm, blocked

Materials
Yarn: super bulky yarn that works to gauge

    Color A (gold), 225yd/206m
    Color B (green), 175yd/160m

Knitting Needles: 8mm (size 11 U.S.) circular
needle 61cm/24" or size to obtain gauge

Tapestry needle to weave in the ends

Gauge
11 st and 16 rows = 4"/10cm over chart pattern

Always take time to check your gauge.

Pattern Stitches
Garter Stitch

Knit every stitch in every row.

Stockinette Stitch

Row 1 and all RS rows: knit all stitches.
Row 2 and all WS rows: purl all stitches.

Repeat rows 1 and 2 for pattern.

Instructions

1. With color A (gold), cast on 59 sts.

2. Work 10 rows in Garter st.

3. Changing colors as indicated in chart, establish patterns:

Work 5 st Garter st, place marker (pm).
Work 49 stitches St st following chart: work sts 1-12 four times then st 13 once.
Pm, work 5 st in Garter st.

4. Continuing to work Garter st borders as established and slipping markers when you come to them, work rows 1-20 of chart 4 times, then rows 1-3 once more. Remember to slip the unused color stitches with the yarn in back on RS rows and the yarn in front on WS rows. (See page 40 for instructions on Mosaic Knitting.)

5. With color A (gold), work 10 rows in Garter st.

6. Bind off.

Finishing

Weave in the ends and block.

This rug was knit with
Classic Elite's *Waterspun Weekend*, 100% Wool,
57yd/52m per skein.

(A) 4 skeins, Chamois #7245
(B) 3 skeins Oasis #7225

Mosaic patterns work equally
well in Stockinette st and
Garter st. If you don't fancy
purling, knit both RS and WS
rows. Your rug will come out
shorter and wider than mine
did, and in an entirely different texture. Test on a swatch
first to make sure you like the
results.

projects **111**

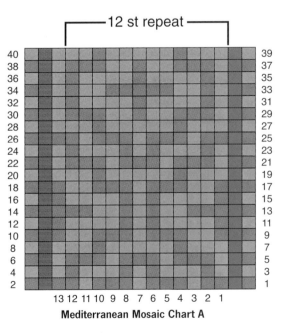

— 12 st repeat —

40 38 36 34 32 30 28 26 24 22 20 18 16 14 12 10 8 6 4 2

39 37 35 33 31 29 27 25 23 21 19 17 15 13 11 9 7 5 3 1

13 12 11 10 9 8 7 6 5 4 3 2 1

Mediterranean Mosaic Chart A

texture rugs

Textured knitting techniques are among my favorites. I love the rhythm that develops as you learn the stitch patterns and relax into them. You can create knitted textures using many different techniques. You've already seen a few simple textures made with knit-and-purl stitch patterns. This section covers techniques that are more elaborate, but not necessarily more difficult.

Felted rugs are intentionally shrunk to make them stronger. By breaking the rules and washing knitted wool in hot water, you can create a thick felt fabric that is indestructible as well as beautiful. The *entrelac*, or *basketweave*, technique creates a texture that looks like strips of knitting have been woven together, but it's actually achieved by knitting one square at a time and attaching them to the previous sections.

Cables provide an almost limitless selection of braids, ropes, and other designs that you can make by simply knitting stitches out of order. With just two basic cable crosses—left and right—this technique is easer than it appears.

If you've ever accidentally shrunk a wool sweater in the wash, you already know how to felt. Felting hides flaws in your knitting, so it's easy to have fun with this technique. Just sew up any misshapen or dropped stitches, and they will disappear as the fibers mat together in the washing machine.

Pastel Felt Rug

Finished Measurements

Approx 34 x 46"/86 x 116cm with crochet edge before felting

Approx 28 x 43"/ 71 x 109cm after felting

Note: The exact finished size is determined by the yarn, your gauge, and felting. I removed this rug from the washer after only a few minutes because I liked the texture of the rug with the Garter ridges still visible. If you felt the rug for a longer period of time, it will get thicker and smaller, and the stitches will disappear.

Materials

Yarn: bulky yarn that will felt (for tips on selecting yarn, see Felting in Special Techniques on page 41)

    Color A (green), 550yd/502m
    Color B (blue), 660yd/604m

Knitting needles: 12mm (size 17 U.S.) circular needles, approx 80cm/32" long, *or size to obtain gauge*

Note: I like the superfast knitting I can achieve on smooth, nickel-plated needles. If you're a new knitter, you might find that wood or bamboo needles give you more control over this loose knitting, and that you'll drop fewer stitches.

Tapestry needle for sewing the two halves together and for weaving in ends

Upholstery needle or awl for making holes in felt to attach tassels

Gauge

Approx 7 sts and 14 rows = 4"/10cm over Garter st, using a double strand of yarn, before felting

Note: For this rug, the exact gauge is not important. Make sure your knitting is loose and there is airy space between stitches. If your stitches seem tight, switch to a larger needle.

Pattern Stitch

Garter Stitch

Knit every stitch of every row.

Instructions

1. With a double strand of color A (green), cast on 80 sts. Work in Garter st for 24 rows.

2. Change to color B (blue) and work in Garter st for 72 rows.

3. Change to color A (green) and work in Garter st for 24 rows.

4. Bind off.

Finishing

With color A (green) work one row of single crochet around the edge of the rug. Work three single crochets into each corner st.

Weave in the loose ends securely so they do not come undone during felting.

Felt (see page 41) and block the rug (see page 52).

Attach tassels to the four corners of the rug after felting. Use an upholstery needle or an awl to make holes in the felt for attaching the tassel if you have trouble getting a tapestry needle to go through the fabric.

Making Variations

You can easily customize this rug by changing the yarn and adding color to create a design that complements your décor.

Changing the yarn for this project takes a little thought. When you felt your rug, the wool fibers will form a strong matted material, so you don't have to worry about selecting a hard-wearing yarn. But you do have to make sure the yarn you select will felt (see page 41).

Choose a plain, plied wool yarn for a smooth, solid rug.

Choose a softly spun singles yarn or a blend of wool and mohair for a fuzzier rug.

Use a strand of wool with a strand of novelty yarn, such as eyelash or boucle, to add texture.

While you can also change the colors of this rug, be careful. Different yarns-and even different colors of the same yarn-may felt differently. When using several colors in one rug, work a generous swatch and felt it as a test.

This rug was knit with
Reynolds' *Lopi*, 100% wool, 110 yd/100m

(A) 5 balls, Pale Willow #0369
(B) 6 balls, Light Blue #0082

design tip

If this rug is a bit too furry for your taste, take a tip from master knitters in the medieval guild—and shear it. Use a dog or cat brush to make the fur on the surface of the felt stand up, and then use very sharp sewing scissors to cut it off to reveal the smooth, dense felt underneath. Be careful not to cut into the actual knitting, though.

Rope Cable Runner

What's exciting about cables is that they look complicated, but are surprisingly easy to knit. With simple rope cables framing a knit-and-purl center, this runner is the perfect project for learning to knit cables. Although the knitting goes fast, the result is so elegant everyone will think it took ages to make.

Finished Measurements
Approx 19 x 60"/48 x 152cm blocked

Note: To make the rug wider, add more stitches in the center panel. To make the rug longer or shorter, work to the desired length. Remember to buy extra yarn if you decide to make a bigger rug.

Materials
Yarn: Medium weight wool or wool-blend yarn

  Colors A (tan), 600 yd/549m
  Color B (beige), 600 yd/549m
  Color C (cream), 600 yd/549m

Knitting needles: 5.75mm (size 10 U.S.) straight or circular needles *or size to obtain gauge*

Cable needle

Row counter

Four stitch markers

Tapestry needle for weaving in ends

Gauge
10 st and 14 rows = 4"/10cm over Rev St st using three strands of yarn held together

Always take time to check your gauge.

Pattern Stitches
Right Cable

Rows 1, 3, and 7 (RS): K6.
Row 2 (and all WS rows): P6.
Row 5: Slip 3 sts to cable needle and hold in back, K3, K3 from cable needle.

Repeat rows 1-8 for pattern.

Left Cable

Rows 1, 3, and 7 (RS): K6.
Row 2 (and all WS rows): P6.
Row 5: Slip 3 sts to cable needle and hold in front, K3, K3 from cable needle.

Repeat rows 1-8 for pattern.

Note: for information on the symbols used in cable charts, see page 32 in Knitting Basics.

Reverse Stockinette Stitch (Rev St st).

Row 1 and all RS rows: Purl all stitches.
Row 2 and all WS rows: Knit all stitches.

Repeat rows 1 and 2 for pattern.

Selvage Stitch:

Knit the first and last stitch of every row to create a clean, crisp edge.

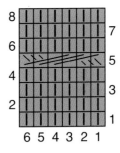

**Rope Cable Runner:
Right Cable**

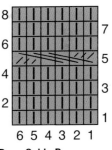

**Rope Cable Runner:
Left Cable**

Instructions

1. CO 50 sts using three strands (one of each color) held together.

2. Work setup row (WS):

K1 (selvage st).
Place marker (pm), p6, pm.
K36 (first row of Rev St st).
pm, p6, pm.
K1 (selvage st).

3. Begin pattern stitches as follows:

K1 (selvage st).
Slip marker (sm), work 6 st right cable chart, sm.
Work Rev St st.
sm, work 6 st left cable chart, sm.
K1 (selvage st).

4. Continue to work patterns as established until rug measures 60"/153cm.

5. End on row 1 of cable charts.

6. Bind off on WS in pattern.

Finishing

Weave in the ends and block.

This rug was knit with
Harrisville's *Highland Style Knitting Yarn,* 200 yd/183m per skein.

3 skeins of each color:

(A) Camel
(B) Sand
(C) White

Felted Basketweave Design

The trick to basketweave knitting, also called entrelac, is to follow the instructions carefully, step by step. You don't have to tell your friends how quickly you learned to make this stunning rug—let them stay amazed!

Finished Measurements
24" x 44"/61 x 112cm before felting

16 x 37"/41 x 94cm after felting, without fringe

Materials
Yarn: bulky weight wool yarn

 Color A (hand-painted), 244yd/223m
 Color B (black), 244yd/223m

Knitting needles: 8mm (size 11 U.S) circular needle, 61cm/24" or longer, *or size to obtain gauge.*

Blunt tapestry needle for weaving in ends

Felting supplies (see page 41).

Gauge
Approx. 12 sts = 4"/10cm over St st before felting

Always take time to check your gauge.

Work from bottom to top of diagram

Top Triangles—worked on RS from right to left

Repeat (Right Leaning Rectangles) one more time

Repeat (Right and Left Leaning Rectangles) six more times

Left Leaning Rectangles—work on RS from right to left

Right Leaning Rectangles with Side Triangles—work on WS from left to right

Base Triangles—work on RS from right to left

Instructions
Base Triangles
Worked on RS from right to left.

1. With color A (hand-painted), loosely cast on 40 sts.

2. Work first triangle:

Row 1 (RS): K2, turn.
Row 2 (WS): P2, turn.
Row 3: K3, turn.
Row 4: P3, turn.
Row 5: K4, turn.
Row 6: P4, turn.
Row 7: K5, turn.
Row 8: P5, turn.
Row 9: K6, turn.
Row 10: P6, turn.
Row 11: K7, turn.
Row 12: P7, turn.
Row 13: K8, turn.
Row 14: P8, turn.
Row 15: K9, turn.
Row 16: P9, turn.
Row 17: K10.

Do not turn. Leave sts on the right needle.

3. Work second, third, and fourth triangles as first triangle. Turn after fourth triangle is complete.

Right-Leaning Rectangles
Worked on WS from left to right.

Note: When you p2tog, purl one st from the new rectangle together with one from the base triangle of the previous row. For instructions on p2tog, see page 35 in Special Techniques.

1. Change to color B (black). Work left edge triangle:

Row 1 (WS): P2, turn.

Row 2 (RS): K2, turn.
Row 3: P into front and back of first st (p1f&b), p2tog, turn.
Row 4: K3, turn.
Row 5: p1f&b, p1, p2tog, turn.
Row 6: K4, turn.
Row 7: p1f&b, p2, p2tog, turn.
Row 8: K5, turn.
Row 9: p1f&b, p3, p2tog, turn.
Row 10: K6, turn.
Row 11: p1f&b, p4, p2tog, turn.
Row 12: K7, turn.
Row 13: p1f&b, p5, p2tog, turn.
Row 14: K8, turn.
Row 15: p1f&b, p6, p2tog, turn.
Row 16: K9, turn.
Row 17: p1f&b, p7, p2tog.

Do not turn. All sts from base triangle have been worked. Leave these sts on the right needle.

2. Work rectangles:

With right needle and WS facing, pick up and purl 10 sts along the other edge of the base triangle. Turn.

(For instructions on picking up stitches, see page 36 in Special Techniques.)

Row 1 (RS): K10, turn.
Row 2 (WS): P9, p2tog, turn.
Rows 3-18: Repeat rows 1 and 2 eight more times.
Row 19: K10, turn.
Row 20: P9, p2tog. Do not turn. All st of next base triangle are worked. Leave these sts on the right needle.

Repeat for second and third rectangles.

3. Work right-side triangle:

With right needle and WS facing, pick up and purl 10 sts along other side of base triangle. Turn.

Row 1 (RS): K10, turn.
Row 2 (WS):P8, p2tog, turn.
Row 3: K9, turn.
Row 4: P7, p2tog, turn.
Row 5: K8, turn.
Row 6: P6, p2tog, turn.
Row 7: K7, turn.
Row 8: P5, p2tog, turn.
Row 9: K6, turn.
Row 10: P4, p2tog, turn.
Row 11: K5, turn.
Row 12: P3, p2tog, turn.
Row 13: K4, turn.
Row 14: P2, p2tog, turn.
Row 15: K3, turn.
Row 16: P1, p2tog, turn.
Row 17: K2, turn,
Row 18: p2tog.

Leave remaining st on right needle. Turn.

Left-Leaning Rectangles
Worked on RS from right to left.

1. Change to color A (hand-painted). With RS facing, slip one st to the right needle, then pick up and knit 9 sts along the edge of the triangle. Turn.

Row 1 (WS): P10, turn.
Row 2 (RS): K9, ssk (see instructions for slip-slip-knit, page 000), turn.
Rows 3-18: Repeat rows 1 and 2 eight more times.
Row 19: P10, turn.
Row 20: K9, ssk.

Do not turn. All sts of next rectangle are worked. Leave these sts on the right needle.

2. Repeat for second, third, and fourth rectangles, picking up 10 sts from the left edge of the next rectangle.

Work right- and left-leaning rectangles six more times, then work right-leaning rectangles one final time. (Pick up stitches as indicated along edges of rectangles instead of base triangles.)

Top Triangles
Worked on RS from right to left.

1. With RS facing, slip one st to the right needle, then, pick up and knit 9 sts along the inside edge of the right-edge triangle. Turn.

Row 1 (WS): P10, turn.
Row 2 (RS): K9, ssk, turn.
Row 3: P8, p2tog, turn.
Row 4: K8, ssk, turn.
Row 5: P7, p2tog, turn.

Row 6: K7, ssk, turn.
Row 7: P6, p2tog, turn.
Row 8: K6, ssk, turn.
Row 9: P5, p2tog, turn.
Row 10: K5, ssk, turn.
Row 11: P4, p2tog, turn.
Row 12: K4, ssk, turn.
Row 13: P3, p2tog, turn.
Row 14: K3, ssk, turn.
Row 15: P2, p2tog, turn.
Row 16: K2, ssk, turn.
Row 17: P1, p2tog, turn.
Row 18: K1, ssk, turn.
Row 19: P2tog, turn.
Row 20: ssk.

Do not turn. Leave remaining st on right needle.

2. Repeat for second, third, and fourth top triangles, first st is already on the right needle.

3. Fasten off the last stitch.

Finishing

Weave in the ends securely.

Felt and block. For instructions, see pages 41 and 52.

Trim or "shear" if desired. (See the Design Tip in the Pastel Felted Rug project on page 115.)

Make two 16"/41cm pieces of knitted cord (see page 44 in Embellishments & Accessories), and sew them to the two ends of the rug.

Attach fringe to the knitted cord (see page 46).

This rug was knit with
Cherry Tree Hill Yarns', *New Zealand Wool* 14-ply, 100% wool, 244yds/223m, per skein

(A) 1 skein, Java
(B) 1 skein, hand-dyed black

Elegant Celtic Cables

SKILL LEVEL
EXPERIENCED

Inspired by drawings in the illuminated medieval Irish manuscript, the *Book of Kells*, this classic Celtic design has unusual cables that start in the middle of plain knitting. The increase and decrease combinations make the cables seem to appear out of nowhere. While not for the faint-of-heart, the resulting rug is so beautiful, it will be a showpiece for many years.

Finished Measurements
Approx. 38 x 38"/97 x 97cm after blocking

Materials
Yarn: super bulky wool yarn

    Color A (light gray), 400yds/366m
    Color B (dark gray), 400yds/366m

Knitting needles: 12mm (size 17 U.S.) circular needle at least 74cm/29"long, *or size needed to obtain gauge.*

Cable needle

2 stitch markers

Tapestry needle for weaving in ends and sewing seams

Gauge
Approx 10 sts and 12 rows = 4"/10 cm over Rev St st

Always take time to check your gauge.

Pattern Stitches
Reverse Stockinette Stitch (Rev St st).

Row 1 and all RS rows: Purl all stitches.
Row 2 and all WS rows: Knit all stitches.

Repeat rows 1 and 2 for pattern.

Garter Stitch
Knit every stitch in every row.

4-st Left Cable

Slip next 2 sts to cable needle and hold in front. K2, k2 from cn.

4-st Right Cable

Slip next 2 sts to cable needle and hold in back. K2, k2 from cn.

Elegant Celtic Cables: Border

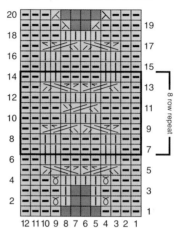

Elegant Celtic Cables: Knot Cable

4-st Left Purl Cable

Slip next 2 knit sts to cable needle and hold in front. P2, k2 from cn.

4-st Right Purl Cable

Slip next 2 purl sts to cable needle and hold in back. K2, p2 from cn.

Note: For information on the symbols used in cable charts, see page 32 in Knitting Basics.

Instructions

Border

1. Cast on 12 sts with color B (dark gray).

2. Work the side:

Row 1 (RS), set up patterns: K2, pm, p8, pm, k2.
Row 2 and even (WS) rows: Knit all stitches, slipping markers when you come to them.
Row 3 and odd (RS) rows: K2, sm, p8, sm, k2. Work in pattern until you have six rows.

Note: Work 2 sts of Garter st at the beginning and end of each row, with 8 sts of Rev St st in the middle.

On next RS row, begin chart A between markers:

K2, sm, work chart A over next 8 sts, sm, k2.

Note: Chart A begins with eight sts and increases to 12 sts in the first four rows. The extra four sts are decreased on rows 19 and 20.

Work rows 1-6 once.
Work rows 7-14 11 times.
Work rows 15-20 once.

Work six rows with 2 sts of Garter st at the beginning and end of each row, and 8 sts of Rev St st in the middle as at the beginning of the side.

3. Work corner:

Continuing in patterns, work 1 less stitch on each RS row (you'll be turning in the middle of the row to make a short row shaping).

When only 1 st remains, begin working 1 more stitch on each RS row. When you have 12 sts, end on a WS row.

Note: The extra stitches are the stitches you left on the needle when you turned in the middle of the short rows.

Repeat side and corner three more times.

Bind off and sew ends together to form a square.

Center

1. Cast on 72 sts with color A (light gray).

2. Work in Rèv St st for 10"/25 cm.

3. Begin chart B: P24, pm, work 24 sts of chart B, pm, p24.

Continue working 24 st in Rev St st on either side of the chart, and work chart B between markers until all rows of chart B have been worked.

Note: Chart B beings with 24 sts, increases to 40 sts for the cables, and decreases back down to 24 sts.

4. Work in Rev St st for 10"/25 cm.

5. Bind off.

Finishing

Sew border around center using whipstitch on RS for decorative seam.

Weave in ends and block.

This rug was knit with
Classic Elite's *Waterspun Weekend*, 100% *Merino Wool*, 57yd/52 m per ball

(A) 7 skeins, Silver #2774
(B) 7 skeins, Charcoal #2772

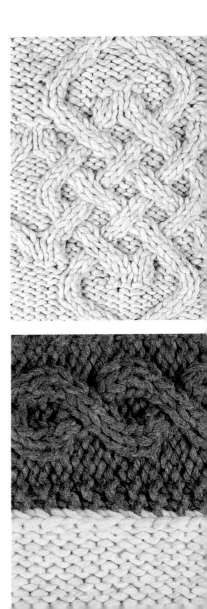

Acknowledgments

Many people helped me turn a simple idea into a beautiful book. I owe each one of them more than I can repay. To Carol Taylor for believing in my idea. To Deborah Morgenthal and Nicole Tuggle for helping me get the project off the ground. To Nathalie Mornu for helping me navigate a seemingly endless stream of paperwork. To Marcianne Miller, my editor, for her encouragement and creative ideas, and for sticking with me through chaos and calm. To Tom Metcalf and Shannon Yokeley for creating such a beautiful book out of a pile of manuscript pages, drawings, and slides. To Orrin Lundgren for having the precision required to translate my illegible handwritten notes into detailed and accurate illustrations. To all of my writing and knitting friends who read and tested each part of the manuscript at every phase. Especially to the ladies in my Wednesday writing group: Kris Bart, Suzanne Hershberger, Cynthia Swan, and Kathy Lenning-Sumpter. To Deborah Robson for not letting me sink into writers block. To each of the designers who contributed rugs to the Gallery for letting me share their work with you. To Suzann Thomson and Priscilla Gibson-Roberts for writing the articles about knitted rugs that inspired me and started me on this fantastic journey. To Artful Yarns, Brown Sheep, Classic Elite, Lion Brand, Halcyon Yarn, Harrisville Yarns, Cherry Tree Hill, La Lana Wools, Peace Fleece, Plymouth, and Reynolds/JCA for contributing yarn for the projects. To JoAnne Turcotte, Mary Drobnis, and Stacey Budge for checking, double-checking, and triple-checking my project instructions. To my mother, Joyce Druchunas, for knitting almost as many rugs as I did. And finally, to my husband, Dominic Cotignola, for taking the photos for the gallery, but mostly for letting me fill our entire house with yarn and rugs for over a year!

Thank you all for your help and encouragement!

Contributing Artists

Fiber artist *Katharine Cobey* creates unique knitted sculpture pieces as well as hand-knit clothing. Katharine teaches workshops in knitting and spinning in her studio in Cushing, Maine. Cushing is a very small village and Katharine's studio is a gallery workspace, a barn-like building on the crest of a hill overlooking a wide tidal estuary. Katharine believes that all knitters are creative and that when we knit our own designs, rather than following directions, we will be better able to knit how and what we choose. The goal of Katherine's workshops is to make knitting clear, and to encourage knitters to work in creative ways.

Judy Dercum has been knitting for almost 50 years, having learned to knit as a   young girl from her mother. Once a national level ski racer, Judy's passions are now hiking and gathering plants for natural dyeing. Today, Judy lives in Colorado where she designs and knits original, one-of-a-kind wearable art, using natural dyes and fibers. Her sweaters, with designs influenced by the landscapes and cultures of the Southwest, have sold to international clients and celebrities. Judy's designs have also been featured in *Knitting in America, Knitter's Stash, Simple Knits, Handpaint Country*, as well as in *Interweave Knits* and *Knitters* magazines.

Master rugmaker *Diana Blake Gray* was named one of America's top 150 traditional craft artists in 1985 for her work in resurrecting and preserving lost techniques of making rag rugs. Her rugs have been exhibited in galleries and museums all over America and sold all over the world. Diana wrote her first book about traditional rug making in 1984, drawing on years of research and experience. By that date she had already made hundreds of rugs using dozens of lost methods. Today, she continues to promote these time-honored crafts, believing that the only way to preserve a folk art is to teach it to others.

Lucy Neatby, owner of Tradewind Knitwear Designs in Nova Scotia, Canada, is a Merchant Navy officer turned award-winning hand-knitting designer and passionate knitting teacher. As well as being a full-time mother to three children, Lucy loves to spend time playing with yarn: intricate color-work and ingenious knitting techniques amuse her for hours on end. She feels very fortunate to be able to do what she loves: knit whatever tickles her fancy, write superbly crafted knitting patterns, and inspire others to new knitting adventures through her workshops.

Carol Rasmussen Noble is a knitwear designer and textile researcher who has published five books on knitting, including *Gossamer Webs, Knitting Fair Isle Mittens and Gloves, Style at Large,* and *Lavish Lace.* She lives in Reno, Nevada with her husband and cat.

Rob Price learned to finger knit at school in the second grade and then taught his mother how to do it. He is now 21 and an artist working primarily in acrylics and prisma colors. Rob is also studying music at South Plains College near Lubbock, Texas. Unfortunately, he doesn't still knit today.

Linda Romens' mother taught her to knit when she was seven years old, using poultry skewers. After this somewhat painful experience, she didn't knit again until she was in college when she attempted her first Fair Isle sweater. After this not-too-successful attempt Linda began knitting in earnest and with more success. Linda's designs have been featured in many books including *Knitting in America* and *Handpaint*

Country, in *Knitters* and *Interweave Knits* magazines, and in the exhibition *Breaking Patterns: Contemporary Hand Knitting in the United States* held in Maryland. She teaches knitting and is also the "knitting guru" at La Lana Wools in Taos, New Mexico.

Suzann Thompson, a fiber artist who recently returned to Texas after living in Sheffield, England for seven years, has a B.A. in Biology, which goes to prove that you don't necessarily need to go to art school to be a designer. Suzann has been a full-time freelance writer and designer since 1993, designing and writing for magazines. Knitting and crochet were her mainstay, while she also experimented with polymer clay and other mediums. Suzann held a solo exhibition at the *Colour Museum* http://www.sdc.org.uk/museum/mus.htm in Bradford, West Yorkshire, England, in 2002, featuring her knitted and quilted wallhangings and garments. Several of her crochet and knitting designs are also on the Web.

Index